H. C. Speer

Laws for the Regulation and Support of Common Schools

With Notes and Forms for School Officers

H. C. Speer

Laws for the Regulation and Support of Common Schools
With Notes and Forms for School Officers

ISBN/EAN: 9783337232474

Printed in Europe, USA, Canada, Australia, Japan

Cover: Foto ©Suzi / pixelio.de

More available books at **www.hansebooks.com**

STATE OF KANSAS.

LAWS

FOR THE

REGULATION AND SUPPORT

OF

COMMON SCHOOLS,

WITH

NOTES AND FORMS FOR SCHOOL OFFICERS.

PUBLISHED JUNE 1, 1881, BY

H. C. SPEER,

STATE SUPERINTENDENT OF PUBLIC INSTRUCTION,
[Under authority of Laws 1879, ch. 166, sec. 84.]

TOPEKA:

COMMON SCHOOLS.

EDUCATIONAL PROVISIONS OF THE ORGANIC ACT.

SECTION 34. *And be it further enacted,* That when the lands in the said territory shall be surveyed under the direction of the government of the United States, preparatory to bringing the same into market, sections numbered sixteen and thirty-six in each township in said territory shall be and the same are hereby reserved for the purpose of being applied to schools in said territory and in the states and territories hereafter to be erected out of the same.

Approved May 30, 1854.

EDUCATIONAL PROVISIONS OF THE STATE CONSTITUTION.

ARTICLE II.

SEC. 23. The legislature, in providing for the formation and regulation of schools, shall make no distinction between the rights of males and females.

ARTICLE VI.

SECTION 1. The state superintendent of public instruction shall have the general supervision of the common-school funds and educational interests of the state, and perform such other duties as may be prescribed by law. A superintendent of public instruction shall be elected in each county, whose term of office shall be two years, and whose duty and compensation shall be prescribed by law.

SEC. 2. The legislature shall encourage the promotion of intellectual, moral, scientific and agricultural improvement, by establishing a uniform system of common schools and schools of higher grade, embracing normal, preparatory, collegiate, and university departments.

SEC. 3. The proceeds of all lands that have been or may be granted by the United States to the state, for the support of schools, and the five hundred thousand acres of land granted to the new states under an act of congress distributing the proceeds of public lands among the several states of the Union, approved September 4, A. D. 1841, and all estates of persons dying without heir or will, and such per cent. as may be granted by congress on the sale of lands in this state, shall be the common property of the state, and shall be a perpetual school fund, which shall not be diminished, but the interest of which, together with all the rents of the lands, and such other means as the legislature may provide by tax or otherwise, shall be inviolably appropriated to the support of common schools.

SEC. 4. The income of the state school funds shall be disbursed annually, by order of the state superintendent, to the several county treasurers, and thence to the treasurers of the several school districts, in equitable proportion to the number of children and youth resident therein, between the ages of five and twenty-one years: *Provided,* That no school district in which a common school has not been maintained at least three months in each year, shall be entitled to receive any portion of such funds.

SEC. 5. The school lands shall not be sold unless such sale be authorized by a vote of the people at a general election; but, subject to revaluation every five years, they may be leased for any number of years not exceeding twenty-five, at a rate established by law.

SEC. 6. All money which shall be paid by persons as an equivalent for exemption from military duty; the clear proceeds of estrays, ownership of which shall vest in the taker-up; and the proceeds of fines for any breach of the penal laws, shall be exclusively applied in the several counties in which the money is paid or fines collected, to the support of common schools.

SEC. 7. Provisions shall be made by law for the establishment, at some eligible and central point, of a state university, for the promotion of literature, and the arts and sciences, including a normal and agricultural department. All funds arising from the sale of lands granted by the United States to the state for the support of a state university, and all other grants, donations or bequests, either by the state or by individuals, for such purpose, shall remain a perpetual fund, to be called the "university fund," the interest of which shall be appropriated to the support of the state university.

SEC. 8. No religious sect or sects shall ever control any part of the common-school or university funds of the state.

SEC. 9. The state superintendent of public instruction, secretary of state and attorney general shall constitute a board of commissioners for the management and investment of the school funds. Any two of said commissioners shall be a quorum.

[*Constitution ratified by the people, October 4, 1859.*]

SEC. 5. No provision has been made by law for the leasing of school lands.

EDUCATIONAL PROVISIONS OF THE ACT OF ADMISSION.

SEC. 3. * * * *First:* That sections numbered sixteen and thirty-six, in every township of public lands in said state, and where either of said sections, or any part thereof, has been sold or otherwise been disposed of, other lands, equivalent thereto, and as contiguous as may be, shall be granted to said state for the use of schools.

Second: That seventy-two sections of land shall be set apart and reserved for the use and support of a state university, to be selected by the governor of said state, subject to the approval of the commissioner of the general land office, and to be appropriated and applied in such manner as the legislature of said state may prescribe for the purpose aforesaid, but for no other purpose.

Approved January 29, 1861.

LAWS RELATING TO COMMON SCHOOLS.

ARTICLE I.— State Superintendent of Public Instruction.

Official Qualification.— Section 1. [Laws 1879, Ch. 166, Sec. 78.] The state superintendent of public instruction shall, before he enters upon the duties of his office, take and subscribe the proper oath of office, and shall execute to the state of Kansas a bond in the sum of ten thousand dollars, with two or more sufficient sureties, to be approved by the executive council, conditional that he shall faithfully perform the duties of his said office, which oath and bond shall be filed in the office of the secretary of state.

General Duties.—SEC. 2. [Laws 1879, Ch. 166, Sec. 79.] The educational interests of the state shall be under the supervision and management of the state superintendent of public instruction, subject to such limitations and restrictions as are or may be prescribed by law; and he shall have and exercise the powers and perform the duties prescribed in the acts relating to common schools.

Assistant Superintendent.—SEC. 3. [Laws 1879, Ch. 166, Sec. 80.] The state superintendent shall have power to appoint an assistant superintendent of public instruction, who shall take the proper oath of office, which shall be filed in the office of the secretary of state; and such assistant shall perform such duties as his principal shall prescribe, not inconsistent with law. Such assistant shall be styled the "assistant state superintendent of public instruction," and the state superintendent shall be responsible for all of the official acts of such assistant. Such superintendent may also appoint an additional clerk, who shall act as clerk of the board of commissioners for the management and investment of the school funds; and such clerk shall perform such other duties as the superintendent may require, and for whose official acts such superintendent shall be responsible.

Apportionment.—SEC. 4. [Laws 1879, Ch. 166, Sec. 81.] Such state superintendent shall distribute the income of the state school fund and the annual taxes collected by the state for the support of common schools to those counties of the state from which the proper reports have been received by said state superintendent. Such distribution shall be made twice in each year, as follows: All such moneys received up to the fifteenth of February shall be distributed between the fifteenth and last day of such month, and that received up to the fifteenth day of August shall be distributed between the fifteenth and last day of such month. The apportionment to each county shall be made in proportion to the number of children over the age of five years and under the age of twenty-one years, resident therein, as shown by the last annual report of the county superintendent to the state superintendent.

SEC. 5 [Laws 1879, Ch. 166, Sec. 82.] Such superintendent shall draw his order on the state treasurer in favor of the county treasurer of the counties respectively entitled to school moneys for the amount of such moneys apportioned to his county, and certify the amount of such order to the state treasurer and state auditor, and also to the county clerk and superintendent of the proper county.

Official Opinions.—SEC. 6. [Laws 1879, Ch. 166, Sec. 83.] Such superintendent shall, at the request of any county superintendent, give his opinion, upon a written statement of the facts, on all questions and controversies arising out of the interpretation and construction of the school laws in regard to the rights, powers and duties of school-district boards, school officers and county superintendents, and shall keep a record of all such decisions. Before giving any such opinion, the superintendent may submit the statement of facts to the attorney general for his advice thereon, and it shall be the duty of the attorney general forthwith to examine such statement, and suggest the proper decision to be made upon such facts.

School Laws and Blanks.—SEC. 7. [Laws 1879, Ch. 166, SEC. 84.] Such superintendent not oftener than once in two years may publish the school laws in force, with such forms, regulations, instructions and decisions as he may judge expedient thereto annexed, and shall cause the same to be forwarded to the persons entitled to receive them. He shall prescribe and cause to be prepared all forms and blanks necessary in the details of the common-school system, so as to secure its uniform operation throughout the state; and shall cause the same to be forwarded to the several county superintendents, to be by them distributed to the several persons or officers entitled to receive the same.

Visitation, and Text-Books.—SEC. 8. [Laws 1879, Ch. 166, Sec. 85.] It shall be the duty of such superintendent to visit each county of the state at least once in two years, and as much oftener as consistent with the discharge of his other duties, for the purpose of advancing and promoting the cause of education throughout the state. It shall be his duty to recommend the most approved text-books for the common schools of the state, and to open such correspondence as may enable him to obtain all necessary information relating to the system of common schools in other states.

Office.—SEC. 9. [Laws 1879, Ch. 166, Sec. 86.] Such superintendent shall have an office in the capitol, where he shall keep all books and papers pertaining to the duties of his office; and all books, school and other, and all apparatus, maps and charts now belonging to the office of the state superintendent, and such as may hereafter be received for such office by purchase, exchange or otherwise, shall be kept and preserved in such office, and delivered by the superintendent to his successor. He shall file and carefully preserve in his office the official reports made to him by the county superintendents of the several counties, trustees or directors of academies, graded schools or colleges.

Copies of Papers.—SEC. 10. [Laws 1879, Ch. 166, SEC. 87.] Copies of all papers filed in his office, and the record of his official acts, may be certified by him, and when so certified shall be evidence equally and in like manner as the originals.

Biennial Report.—SEC. 11. [Laws 1879, Ch. 166, Sec. 88.] The superintendent shall, on the first day of December preceding each regular session of the legislature, make out and deliver to the governor a report containing —

First: A statement of the number of common schools in the state, the number of scholars attending the same, their sex, and the branches taught; a statement of the number of private or select schools in the state, so far as the same can be ascertained, and the number of scholars attending the same, their sex, and the branches taught; a statement of the number of normal schools in the state, and the number of students attending them; the number of academies and colleges in the state, and the number of students, and their sex, attending them; and such other matters of interest as he may deem expedient, drawn from the reports of the county superintendents of the several counties in the state, and from other reports received on the subject of education from trustees or other school boards within the state.

Second: A statement of the condition of the common-school fund of the state, including moneys, school lands or other property held in trust by the state for the support of common schools, and giving a full statement of the school-land account of each county.

Third: A statement of the receipts and expenditures for the year.

Fourth: A statement of plans for the management and improvement of common schools; and such other information relating to the educational interests of the state as he may deem important.

ARTICLE II.— COUNTY SUPERINTENDENT.

Oath and Bond.—SECTION 12. [Laws 1881, Ch. 152, Sec. 1.] The county superintendent of public instruction shall, before he enters upon the duties of his office, take and subscribe an oath or affirmation to support the constitution of the United States and of the state of Kansas; to faithfully discharge the duties of such office, and execute to the state of Kansas a bond in the sum of one thousand dollars, conditioned to the faithful performance of his official duties; which bond, after having been approved by the board of county commissioners, together with his official oath, shall be filed in the office of the county clerk.

General Duties.—Sec. 13. [Laws 1881, Ch. 152, Sec. 2.] It shall be the duty of the county superintendent of public instruction to visit each school in his county at least once each term of six months, correcting any deficiency that may exist in the government of the school, the classification of the pupils, or the methods of instruction in the several branches taught; to make such suggestions in private to the teachers as he shall deem proper and necessary to the welfare of the school; to note the character and condition of the school house, furniture, apparatus and grounds, and make a report in writing to the district board, making such suggestions as in his opinion shall improve the same; to examine the accounts and record books of the district officers, and see that they are kept as required by law; to encourage the formation of associations of teachers and educators for mutual improvement, and, as far as possible, to attend the meetings of such associations, and participate in the exercises of the same; to attend the normal held in his county, using his influence to secure the attendance of teachers; to make daily a personal inspection of the work of the institute in session, and keep a record of the same in his office, and do such work in connection with the exercises of the institute as he may deem necessary; to hold a public meeting in each school district of his county at least once every year, for the purpose of discussing school questions and elevating the standard of education; to keep his office open at the county seat, Saturday of each week, and in counties in which the county superintendent receives a salary of more than six hundred dollars per annum, he shall keep his office open when not necessarily absent attending to his official duties. He shall keep a complete record of his official acts; a record of the name, age and post-office address of each candidate for a teacher's certificate, with the number of weeks said candidate has attended a normal school or institute, the number of weeks he has taught, his standing in each

---

Sec. 13. (a) "At least once each term of six months" is held to mean at least once each half-year.

(b) The power to correct deficiencies in government, classification and methods of instruction, implies a direct responsibility of the teacher to the superintendent. The language of the law is clearly intended to establish this relation somewhat as it exists in city schools. Failure to pay reasonable attention to the suggestions of the county superintendent in these matters is held to be sufficient ground for withholding the teacher's certificate.

(c) The county superintendent cannot receive compensation for work in connection with the normal institute.

(d) The provisions of this section require the entire time of every county superintendent receiving a salary of over six hundred dollars.

study, and the date of issue and expiration of each certificate granted. He shall keep a register of the teachers employed in his county, giving name of teacher, number of the district in which he is employed, dates of opening and closing term, salary per month, grade of certificate, and date of superintendent's visit. He shall keep a record of the semi-annual apportionments of the state and county school funds, and such other statistical records as shall be required in making reports to the state superintendent of public instruction. He shall make out and transmit to the state superintendent, on the last Monday of March, June, September and December of each year, a report, showing the number of school visits made, with the average length of time spent in such visits; the number of consultations held with school officers; the number of days his office has been kept open; the number of district treasurers' and clerks' record books examined; the number of teachers' meetings attended; the number of public lectures delivered; and such other information as the state superintendent may require regarding the duties of such county superintendent; and until such report shall have been forwarded to the state superintendent, and a copy thereof filed with the county clerk for publication, and that fact certified by the said county superintendent to the board of county commissioners, the warrant for his salary shall not be drawn. The county superintendent shall obtain from the county clerk, at least ten days before the time for holding the annual school meeting each year, a certified statement of the total assessed valuation of the property in each school district in his county, and immediately certify the same to the several school-district clerks of his county, for the information of the annual school meeting; and it is hereby made the duty of said county clerks to make out said certified statement, and deliver the same to the county superintendent.

Apportionment of School Funds.—SEC. 14. [Laws 1881, Ch. 152, Sec. 3.] Within five days after receiving the certificate of the state superintendent of public instruction, informing him of the amount of state school fund which has been apportioned to his county, the county superintendent shall apportion the same, together with the unapportioned county school fund in the county treasury, among the school districts and parts of districts in such county, in the ratio of the number of per

SEC. 14. A district must not only have had a common school taught at least three months during the school year ending July 31st; it must also have made through its district clerk, the requisite annual report for the school year in time to be included in the annual report of the county superintendent, or the county superintendent cannot legally apportion to the district a share of the next ensuing February and August dividends of the state and county school funds. In apportioning these funds the county superintendent must be governed not only by the proviso regarding the length of school term, but also by the *number* of children of school age residing in the several districts of the county, "*as the same shall appear from the last annual reports of the clerks of the respective districts.*" For purposes of apportionment, it is only from the annual report of the clerk of a district that the county superintendent can *legally* know the number of children of school age residing in the district.

sons of school age residing in each district or part of district, as shown by the last annual reports of the several clerks of such districts and parts of districts: *Provided,* That no district in which a common school has not been taught at least three months the last preceding school year shall be entitled to receive any portion of either of said funds; and he shall draw his order on the county treasurer in favor of each of the several school-district treasurers for the amount apportioned to such district.

School-District Boundaries.—Sec. 15. [Laws 1881, Ch. 152, Sec. 4.] It shall be the duty of the county superintendent of public instruction, on or before the fourth Monday of July of each year, to furnish the clerk of his county a description of the boundaries of each and every school district and part of district in such county.

Annual Report.—Sec. 16. [Laws 1881, Ch. 152, Sec. 5.] He shall, on or before the fifteenth of October of each year, make out and transmit in writing to the state superintendent of public instruction a report bearing date October 1st, containing a statement of the number of school districts or parts of districts in the county, and the number of children and their sex, resident in each, over the age of five and under the age of twenty-one years; a statement of the number of district schools in the county, the length of time a school has been taught in each, the number of scholars attending the same, their sex, the branches taught and the text-books used, the number of teachers employed in the same, and their sex; a statement of the number of private or select schools in the county so far as the same can be ascertained, and the number of teachers employed in the same, their sex, and the branches taught; a statement of the number of graded schools in the county, the length of time school has been taught in each, and the number of scholars attending the same, their sex, and the branches taught, the number of teachers employed in the same, and their sex; a statement of the condition of the normal school, where such school has been established, the number of students attending the same, their sex, and the number of teachers employed in the same, and their sex; a statement of the county normal institute; a statement of the number of academies

---

In the case of the organization of a school district out of a part of the territory of another which is entitled to a portion of the state and county school funds, the newly-formed district should be apportioned its just share of the funds to which the original district would have been entitled. If the division of the district was made before the time of making the annual report, the report of the new district should show the number of children resident of the territory detached from the old district; so that this apportionment may be made upon official returns. If the new district was organized after the time of making the annual report, the officers of the former district should be directed to pay to the treasurer of the new district that portion of the funds to which the children residing upon the detached territory entitle said district.

Sec. 16. The annual reports of county superintendents constitute the basis on which the state superintendent disburses the semi-annual dividends to the several counties. If any county superintendent, therefore, fails to make his annual report, as required by law, the county loses its share of the state school fund, and the county superintendent becomes responsible to the county for the amount.

and colleges in the county, and the number of students attending the same and their sex, the number of teachers employed in each, and their sex ; a statement of the amount of public money received in each district or parts of districts, and what portion of the same, if any, has been appropriated to the support of graded schools ; a statement of the amount of money raised in each district by tax and paid for teachers' wages, in addition to the public money paid therefor ; the amount of money raised by tax or otherwise for the purpose of purchasing school site, for building, hiring, purchasing, repairing, furnishing, or insuring such school house, or for any other purpose allowed by law, in the district or parts of districts.

Compensation.—SEC. 17. [Laws 1881, Ch. 152, Sec. 6.] The county superintendent of public instruction in counties containing one thousand and not more than twelve hundred persons, between the ages of five and twenty-one years, shall receive four hundred dollars per annum ; in counties having a school population of from twelve hundred to fifteen hundred, he shall receive five hundred dollars per annum ; and in counties containing more than fifteen hundred persons of school age, he shall receive five hundred dollars, and twenty dollars for each additional one hundred such persons per annum ; in counties having a school population of less than one thousand, the county superintendent shall receive three dollars for each day actually and necessarily employed in the discharge of the duties of his office, for a number of days not to exceed one hundred in any one year, which compensation shall be payable quarterly, on the order of the board of county commissioners : *Provided,* That no county superintendent shall receive to exceed one thousand dollars per annum, and that in determining the salaries of county superintendents, the school population of cities of the first and second class shall not be included.

Vacancy in Board.—SEC. 18. [Laws 1881, Ch. 152, Sec. 7.] Should a vacancy occur in the board of directors of any school district, it shall be the duty of the county superintendent to appoint some suitable person, a resident of the district, to fill the same, and the person so appointed shall continue in office until the next annual meeting thereafter, and until his successor is elected and qualified.

Vacancy in Office of County Superintendent.—SEC. 19. [Laws 1881, Ch. 152, Sec. 8.] When a vacancy occurs in the office of county superintendent of public instruction, by death, resignation or otherwise,

SEC. 17. "School population" is held to mean the enumeration taken annually by school district clerks for the annual report. Such enumeration for each year should constitute the basis for the superintendent's salary for the next year, beginning January 1.

SEC. 18. No petition is required.

notice thereof shall be given by the county clerk to the board of county commissioners, who shall as soon as practicable appoint some suitable person to fill the vacancy, and the person receiving such appointment shall, before entering upon the discharge of the duties of the office, file his oath or affirmation and bond in the county clerk's office as hereinbefore provided, and shall hold his office until his successor is elected and qualified.

Clerks' Reports.—SEC. 20. [Laws 1881, Ch. 152, Sec. 9.] He shall see that the annual reports of the clerks of the several school districts and parts of districts in his county are made correctly and in due time.

Oaths.—SEC. 21. [Laws 1881, Ch. 152, Sec. 10.] County superintendents shall have power to administer oaths in all cases in which an oath is made necessary by any provisions of the school law, except in the qualifying of county superintendents and their sureties.

Purchase of Records.—SEC. 22. [Laws 1881, Ch. 152, Sec. 11.] The county superintendent of public instruction of the respective counties in this state may purchase for each organized school district in his county not having sufficient records, one set of school-district records, consisting of district clerks' records and order books, district treasurer's book, and a teachers' daily register. Each of said books shall contain such printed forms and instructions as will enable the teacher and the school-district officers to perform with correctness and accuracy their several duties as required by law: *Provided,* The entire set of said records as above enumerated shall not exceed in cost four dollars for each set; and the said superintendent shall draw his order or warrant on the county treasurer, in favor of the person he purchases said books of, for the amount of the purchase-money, and it is hereby made the duty of said county treasurer to pay said warrant or order out of any money in his hands belonging to the respective districts in his county: *Provided,* That no funds in the hands of the county treasurer belonging to the several school districts in his county shall be diverted from the object for which said fund was raised, and the said superintendent shall deliver the said books to the district board of each district.

Forming and Changing Districts.—SEC. 23. [Laws 1881, Ch. 152, Sec. 12.] It shall be the duty of the county superintendent of public instruction to divide the county into a convenient number of school districts, and to change such districts when the interests of the inhabitants

---

SEC. 22. There is no warrant of law for purchasing and holding supplies of record books to be delivered to districts as they may be needed. The purchase should be made directly for each district, and warrant drawn against moneys credited to that district on the books of the county treasurer.

SEC. 23. It is very desirable that the people concerned should be consulted, and the arguments on both sides carefully considered, before making important changes. After a district has issued bonds to build or purchase a school house, alterations should be discouraged until the bonds are paid, except in

thereof require it, but only after twenty days' notice thereof, by written notices posted in at least five public places in the district to be changed; but no new school district shall be formed containing less than fifteen persons of school age, no district shall be so changed as to reduce its school population to less than fifteen, and none having a bonded indebtedness shall be so reduced in territory that such indebtedness shall exceed five per cent. of their assessed property valuation : *Provided*, That any person interested may appeal to the board of county commissioners from the action of the county superintendent. Such superintendent shall number school districts when they are formed, and he shall keep in a book for that purpose a description of the boundaries of each school district and part of district in his county, with plat of the same, date of organization, date and full record of all changes of boundaries, and a list of district officers in his county, the date of election or appointment, and the time the term of each is to expire.

Notice of First Meeting.—SEC. 24. [Laws 1881, Ch. 152, Sec. 13.] Whenever a school district shall be formed in any county, the county superintendent of public instruction of such county shall within fifteen days thereafter prepare a notice of the formation of such district, describing its boundaries and stating the number thereof. He shall cause the notices thus prepared to be posted in at least five public places in the district, and in case there shall be no appeal, shall in ten days thereafter in like manner appoint a time and place for a special district meeting, for the election of officers and the transaction of such business as is prescribed by law for special school-district meeting.

Other Duties.—SEC. 25. [Laws 1881, Ch. 152, Sec. 14.] He shall discharge such other duties as may be prescribed by law, and in cases of sickness or temporary absence he may employ a deputy. He shall deliver to his successor, within ten days after the expiration of his term of office, all books and papers appertaining to his office.

Neglect or Refusal to Perform Duty.—SEC. 26. [Laws 1881, Ch. 152, Sec. 15.] Every county superintendent who shall neglect or refuse to perform any act which it is his duty to perform, or shall corruptly or oppressively perform any such duty, he shall forfeit his office, and shall be liable on his official bond for all damages occasioned thereby, to be recovered in the name of the state for the benefit of the proper party, district or county.

cases where imperative necessity demands a change. The object should be, to establish strong and permanent districts. It is better for a youth to walk double the distance to a good school, than to have a poor school near his door.

In changing district boundaries, five notices, posted for twenty days preceding, must be given to each district affected. Appeals need not be made from the contemplated action outlined in the twenty-day notices, but must be taken within ten days from the actual change made.

ARTICLE III.—School Districts.

Organization.—Section 27. [Laws 1876, Ch. 122, Art. 3, Sec. 1.] Every school district shall be deemed duly organized when the officers constituting the district board shall have been elected and qualified, and shall have signified their acceptance to the county superintendent in writing, which the superintendent shall file in his office.

Body Corporate.—Sec. 28. [Laws 1876, Ch. 122, Art. 3, Sec. 2.] Every school district organized in pursuance of this act shall be a body corporate, and shall possess the usual powers of a corporation for public purposes, by the name and style of school district No. —— (such a number as may be designated by the county superintendent), ——, county (the name of the county in which the district is situated), state of Kansas, and in that name may sue and be sued, and be capable of contracting and being contracted with, and holding such real and personal estate as it may come into possession of by will or otherwise, or as is authorized to be purchased by the provisions of this act.

Joint Districts.—Sec. 29. [Laws 1879, Ch. 158, Sec. 1.] When it shall become necessary to form a school district, lying partly in two or more counties, the county superintendents of the counties in which the said tract of country shall be situated, when application shall be made in writing to any one of them by five householders resident therein, shall, if by them deemed necessary, meet and proceed to lay off and form the same into a school district, issue notices for the first district meeting, and shall file the proper papers in their respective offices; and such district so organized shall be designated joint district No. ——, counties of ——; and the boundaries of such district shall not be altered except by the joint action of the superintendents of the several counties represented in said district: *Provided,* That if in the alteration of, or refusal to alter, the boundaries of any joint school district, any person or persons shall feel aggrieved, such person or persons may appeal to the state superintendent of public instruction, and notice of such appeal

---

Sec. 27. Officers elected at first district meeting hold only until the next annual election.

Sec. 29. It is held that appeals should be taken to the State Superintendent, in the case of the *formation,* as well as alteration, of joint school districts.

shall be served on the superintendents of the several counties represented in said district within ten days after the rendition by them of the decision appealed from, which notice shall be in writing, and shall state fully the objections to the action of the county superintendent, and a copy thereof shall be filed with the state superintendent of public instruction; and it shall be the duty of the county superintendent in whose possession are the papers connected with the action appealed from to transmit the same to the state superintendent of public instruction, immediately upon being served with notice of appeal, as hereinbefore presented; and thereupon the state superintendent of public instruction shall fix a time for the hearing of said appeal, and notify the several county superintendents interested, and the appellants, thereof; and his decision on said appeal shall be final, and shall be by him certified to the several county superintendents interested, and they shall take action in accordance therewith : *And provided further,* That each joint district, except in matters relating to the alteration of the boundaries thereof, shall be under the jurisdiction and control of the superintendent of that one of the counties represented in such district which has the largest amount of territory embraced within the boundaries of such joint district.

Division of Property.—SEC. 30. [Laws 1876, Ch. 122, Art. 3, Sec. 4.] When a new district is formed, in whole or in part, from one or more districts possessing a school house or entitled to other property, the county superintendent, at the time of forming such new district, shall equitably determine the proportion of the present value of such school house, or other property justly due to said new district. Such proportion, when ascertained, shall be levied by the district board of the district retaining the school house or other property, upon the taxable property of the district, and shall be collected in the same manner as if the same had been authorized by a vote of the district for building a school house, and when collected shall be paid to the treasurer of the new district, to be applied towards procuring a school house for such district.

SEC. 30. For the division of school property under the provisions of this section, the following rules are recommended, viz.:

1ST RULE, *To be applied in dividing school property which has been procured with the proceeds of district taxes:*

First: Find the assessed valuation of the taxable property of the undivided district as returned on the last assessment roll of the county.

Second: Find, in like manner, the *assessed valuation* of the taxable property of the territory which is to be cut off, and which does not retain the school property.

Third: Find the *present value* of the school property of the undivided district, including moneys raised from district taxes and remaining in the treasury at the time the division is made, after discharging all indebtedness payable out of such moneys.

Fourth: Multiply the present value of the school property by the assessed valuation of the territory which is to be cut off. The product divided by the assessed valuation of the undivided district gives the amount due to the territory which is to be cut off.

Aggrieved Persons.—SEC. 31. [Laws 1876, Ch. 122, Art. 3, Sec. 5.] If, in the formation or alteration of, or refusal to form or alter school districts, any person or persons shall feel aggrieved, such person or persons may appeal to the board of county commissioners, who shall confer with the county superintendent, and their action shall be final: *Provided,* That notice of such appeal shall be served on the county superintendent within ten days of the time of posting of the notices of the formation or alteration of such district; such notice shall be in writing, and shall state fully the objections to the action of the county superintendent, a copy of which shall be filed with the county clerk, and also with the clerks of all districts affected by such alteration: *And provided, also,* That such appeal shall be heard and decided by the majority of the board of county commissioners at their next regular meeting; and if such appeal is not sustained by them, the county superintendent shall proceed to appoint the time and place for said first district meeting, which shall then proceed as by law required.

Annual and Special Meetings.—SEC. 32. [Laws 1876, Ch. 122, Art. 3, Sec. 6.] An annual meeting of each school district shall be held on the second Thursday of August of each year, at the school house belonging to the school district, at two o'clock P. M. Notice of the time and place of said annual meeting shall be given by the clerk, by posting written or printed notices in three public places of the district at least ten days before said meeting. Special meetings may be called by the district board, or by a majority of the legal voters of the district, but

2D RULE, *To be applied in dividing such school property as consists of moneys received by the undivided district from the state and county school funds:*

First: Find the number of children of school age residing in the undivided district, as given in the last annual report of the clerk of the district.

Second: Find, in like manner, the number of children of school age residing in the territory which is to be cut off, and which does not retain the school property.

Third: Find the amount of state and county school moneys remaining in the treasury of the undivided district at the time the division is made, after discharging all indebtedness for teachers' wages.

Fourth: Multiply the residue of state and county school moneys by the number of children residing in the territory which is to be cut off. That product divided by the number of children of school age residing in the undivided district, gives the amount of state and county school moneys due to the territory which is to be cut off.

The county superintendent of public instruction should make the division of school property *at the time* of forming a new school district, but his failure to do so at that time does not impair the rights of said district. Within a reasonable time after the organization of a new district, aggrieved parties may demand of him that he make an equitable division of the school property of the original district. Should he neglect or refuse to grant their request, they may, by mandamus, compel him to do so. If an unfair division is made by the county superintendent, either party has a right to appeal to the courts and have the matter adjudicated. If after the division has been made, the officers of the district retaining the school house or other property shall neglect or refuse to levy the tax mentioned in this section, they can be compelled by mandamus to make the levy.

When a new district has been formed, and the county superintendent has determined the amount due the new district from the old, the district retaining the school house *cannot issue bonds* with which to pay the sum due, but must levy a tax as is provided for in this section.

SEC. 31. See note on section 29.

notice of such special meeting, stating the purpose for which it is called, shall be posted in at least three public places within the district ten days previous to the time of such meeting.

Special Meeting.—SEC. 33. [Laws 1876, Ch. 122, Art. 3, Sec. 7.] Whenever the time for holding an annual meeting in any district shall pass without said meeting being held, the clerk, or, in his absence, any other member of the district board, within twenty days after the time for holding said annual meeting shall have passed, may give notice of a special meeting by putting up written notices thereof in three public places within the district, at least five days previous to the time of meeting; but if such meeting shall not be notified within twenty days as aforesaid, the county superintendent may give notice of such meeting in the manner provided for forming new districts; and the officers chosen at such special meeting shall hold their offices until the next annual meeting, and until their successors are elected and qualified.

Notice of Meetings.—SEC. 34. [Laws 1876, Ch. 122, Art. 3, Sec. 8.] It shall be the duty of the clerk to give at least ten days' notice previous to any annual or special district meeting, by posting up notices thereof at three or more public places in the district, one of which notices shall be affixed to the outer door of the school house, if there be one in the district, and said clerk shall give the like notice of every adjourned meeting, when such meeting shall have been adjourned for a longer period than one month. Every notice for a special district meeting shall specify the objects for which such meeting is called, and no business shall be acted upon at any special meeting not specified in said notice.

Qualified Voters.—SEC. 35. [Laws 1876, Ch. 122, Art. 3, Sec. 9.] The following persons shall be entitled to vote at any district meeting:

First — All persons possessing the qualifications of electors as defined by the constitution of the state, and who shall be residents of the district at the time of offering to vote at said election.

Second — All female persons over the age of twenty-one years, not subject to the disqualifications named in section second, article fifth, of the constitution of the state, and who shall be residents of the district at the time of offering to vote.

Challenge.—SEC. 36. [Laws 1876, Ch. 122, Art 3, Soo. 10.] If any person offering to vote at a school-district meeting shall be challenged as unqualified by any legal voter, the chairman presiding shall declare to

---

SEC. 32. This section fixes the time and place of holding the annual meeting of the school district. While it is the *duty* of the district clerk to post the notices of the meeting provided for in the section, a failure to do so will not invalidate the proceedings had, should the voters convene at the proper time and place, and transact the business mentioned in sections 37 and 38 of this article. However, should the district clerk, for any reason, fail to post the notices at the proper time, he should do so as soon thereafter as possible before the second Thursday of August.

the person challenged the qualifications of a voter, and if such challenge be not withdrawn, the chairman, who is hereby authorized, shall tender to the person offering to vote the following oath or affirmation: "You do solemnly swear (or affirm) that you are an actual resident of this school district, and that you are qualified by law to vote at this meeting." Any person taking such oath or affirmation shall be entitled to vote on all questions voted upon at such meeting.

Powers of District Meetings.—SEC. 37. [Laws 1876, Ch. 122, Art. 3, Sec. 11.] The inhabitants qualified to vote at a school meeting, lawfully assembled, shall have power:

First—To appoint a chairman to preside over said-meeting in the absence of the director.

Second—To adjourn from time to time.

Third—To choose a director, clerk, and treasurer, who shall possess the qualifications of voters.

Fourth—To designate, by vote, a site for the district school house.

Fifth—To vote a tax annually, not exceeding one per cent. on the taxable property in the district, as the meeting shall deem sufficient, to purchase or lease a site: *Provided,* When not included within the limits of a town or village, said site shall not contain less than one acre; and to build, hire or purchase such school house, and to keep in repair and furnish the same with the necessary fuel and appendages.

Sixth—To vote a direct tax annually, not exceeding one per cent. of the taxable property in the district, for the pay of teachers' wages in the district.

Seventh—To authorize and direct the sale of any school-house site, or other property belonging to the district, when the same shall no longer be needful for the use of the district.

Eighth—To give such direction and make such provisions as may be deemed necessary in relation to the prosecution or defense of any suit or proceeding in which the district may be a party.

School Term.—SEC. 38. [Laws 1876, Ch. 122, Art. 3, Sec. 12.] The qualified voters at each annual meeting, or any special meeting duly called, may determine the length of time a school shall be taught in their district for the then ensuing year, which shall not be less than three months, and whether such school shall be taught by a male or female teacher, or both, and whether the school money to which the district may be entitled shall be applied to the support of the summer or winter term of the school, or a certain portion to each; but if such mat-

---

SEC. 37. A tax may also be levied for the purpose of purchasing a district library. See Article VIII, section 113.

SEC. 38. The electors, at the annual or a special meeting, have no power to determine who shall or shall not be employed as teacher, or the compensation such teacher shall receive. These are questions to be determined by the district board.

ters shall not be determined at the annual or any special meeting, it shall' be the duty of the district board to determine the same.

Change of Site.—Sec. 39. [Laws 1874, Ch. 122, Sec. 1.] That [in] school districts having school houses the value of which is not less than four hundred dollars, the school-house site shall not be changed except by a vote of at least two-thirds of the legal voters of the district in favor of such change.

Appraisement.—Sec. 40. [Laws 1874, Ch. 122, Sec. 2.] The value of school houses in districts desiring to change the school site shall be determined by three appraisers, who shall be freeholders, chosen at a district meeting by the qualified electors of the district.

Site Condemned.—Sec. 41. [Laws 1874, Ch. 122, Sec. 3.] In case any school district cannot otherwise obtain title to the site selected by such school district, it shall be the duty of the probate judge of the county in which such school-house site is located to appoint three disinterested freeholders to appraise and condemn such site—not to exceed one acre; and such appraisers shall proceed to assess and condemn such site, and upon payment by said district board of such appraisement the title to such site shall vest in said district: *Provided,* That such district board or the owner of the land so condemned shall be entitled to an appeal from such appraisement in such manner and upon such conditions as appeals are made from decisions of justices of the peace.

ARTICLE IV.—District Officers.

Officers; Term.—SECTION 42. [Laws 1876, Ch. 122, Art. 4, Sec. 1.] The officers of each school district shall be a director, clerk, and treasurer, who shall constitute the district board, and who shall be elected and hold their respective offices as follows: At the annual meeting in eighteen hundred and seventy-four there shall be elected a director who shall hold his office for three years, and a clerk who shall hold his office for two years, and a treasurer who shall hold his office for one year; and thereafter at each annual meeting there shall be elected one member of said board in place of the outgoing member, who shall hold his office for three years and until his successor shall be elected and qualified.

Official Oath.—SEC. 43. [Laws 1876, Ch. 122, Art. 4, Sec. 2.] School-district officers, before entering upon their official duties, shall take an oath to faithfully perform said duties; and the chairman of any regular or special meeting is hereby authorized and empowered to administer such oath.

Office Forfeited.—SEC. 44. [Laws 1876, Ch. 122, Art. 4, Sec. 2.] Every person duly elected to the office of director, clerk or treasurer of any school district, who shall refuse or neglect, without sufficient cause, to qualify within twenty days after his election or appointment, or who having entered upon the duties of his office, shall neglect or refuse to perform any duty required of him by the provisions of this act, shall thereby forfeit his right to the office to which he was elected or appointed, and the county superintendent shall thereupon appoint a suitable person in his stead.

Director.—SEC. 45. [Laws 1876, Ch. 122, Art. 4, Sec. 4.] The director of each district shall preside at all district meetings, and shall sign all orders drawn by the clerk, authorized by a district meeting or by the district board, upon the treasurer of the district, for moneys collected or received by him to be disbursed therein. He shall appear for and in behalf of the district, in all suits brought by or against the district, unless other direction shall be given by the voters of such district, at a district meeting.

Clerk.—SEC. 46. [Laws 1876, Ch. 122, Art. 4, Sec. 5.] The clerk of each district shall record the proceedings of his district in a book pro-

SEC. 42. The officers of a school district constitute the board of directors in such a sense as to be able to transact the school business of the district *only when in session as a district board.* As the law is silent as to how, when and where the district board shall be convened, each board should adopt a set of rules for its own government.

Under the provisions of this section, a treasurer should be elected at the annual meeting in August, 1881.

SEC. 43. A district officer can qualify before the chairman of a district meeting, the county superintendent, or any one authorized by law to administer oaths, as a justice of the peace, or notary.

SEC. 44. A county superintendent cannot remove a district officer. Such removal can be made only by an action brought in court. The vacancy being declared, the county superintendent shall appoint. No petition is required.

vided by the district for that purpose, and enter therein copies of all reports made by him to the county superintendent; and he shall keep and preserve all records, books and papers belonging to his office, and deliver the same to his successor in office.

Clerk of the Board.—SEC. 47. [Laws 1876, Ch. 122, Art. 4, Sec. 6.] The said clerk shall be clerk of the district board and of all district meetings, when present; but if such clerk shall not be present at any district meeting, the voters present may appoint a clerk of such meeting, who shall certify the proceedings thereof, and the same shall be recorded by the clerk of the district.

Draw Orders.—SEC. 48. [Laws 1876, Ch. 122, Art. 4, Sec. 7.] The clerk of the district shall draw orders on the treasurer of the district for moneys in the hands of such treasurer which have been apportioned to or raised by the district, to be applied to the payment of teachers' wages, and apply such money to the payment of the wages of such teachers as shall have been employed by the district board; and said clerk shall draw orders on the said treasurer for moneys in the hands of such treasurer to be disbursed for any other purpose ordered by a district meeting or by the district board, agreeably to the provisions of this act.

Annual Report.—SEC. 49. [Laws 1876, Ch. 122, Art. 4, Sec. 8.] The clerk of each district shall, at least five days previous to the time of the annual meeting in August in each year, make a written report, which he shall submit and read to the legal voters of the district at the annual meeting, for their information and consideration. If any change or alteration therein be necessary, the same shall be made, and it shall then be transmitted to the county superintendent of public instruction. Said report shall show: First, the number of children, male or female, designated separately, residing in the district or part of district on the last day of July previous to the date of such report, over the age of five and under the age of twenty-one years; second, the number of children attending school during the year, their sex, and branches studied; third, the length of time a school has been taught in the district by a qualified teacher, the name of the teacher, the length of time taught, and wages paid; fourth, the amount of money received from the county treasurer, arising from disbursement of the state annual school fund, the amount received from district taxes, and the amount received from all other sources during the year, and the manner in which the same has been ex-

---

SEC. 47. In transacting the school business of the district, the members of the board should meet as a district board, the clerk making a complete record of all proceedings.

SEC. 48. Should the director or other member of the board refuse to sign a legal order, payable to any party legally entitled to receive it, such officer may be compelled, by writ of mandamus, to sign.

pended; fifth, the amount of money raised by the district in such year, and the purposes for which it was raised; sixth, the kind of books used in the school, and such other facts and statistics in regard to the district school as the county superintendent may require.

Joint District.—SEC. 50. [Laws 1876, Ch. 122, Art. 4, Sec. 9.] Whenever a school district shall lie partly in two or more counties, the clerk of such district, in making his annual report, shall carefully designate the number of children resident in the parts of the counties composing the district, and shall report to the county superintendent of public instruction of each of the counties in which such district may be partly situated.

Penalty.—SEC. 51. [Laws 1876, Ch. 122, Art. 4, Sec. 10.] Every clerk of a district who shall willfully sign a false report to the county superintendent of his county shall be deemed guilty of a misdemeanor, and punished by a fine not exceeding one hundred dollars, or by imprisonment not exceeding three months.

Report to County Clerk.—SEC. 52. [Laws 1876, Ch. 122, Art. 4, Sec. 11.] It shall be the duty of the several district clerks in this state to make out a certified list of all persons residing within their respective districts liable to pay taxes, and transmit the same to the county clerks of their respective counties on or before the 25th day of August, annually, except in incorporated cities.

Failure to Report.—SEC. 53. [Laws 1876, Ch. 122, Art. 4, Sec. 12.] Any district clerk who shall fail to report the tax voted by his district to the county clerk, as is provided by law, shall be liable to a fine of not less than fifty dollars; and it is hereby made the duty of the county superintendent to have the provisions of this act enforced.

Other Reports.—SEC. 54. [Laws 1876, Ch. 122, Art. 4, Sec. 13.] The district clerk shall report to the county superintendent, in writing, the names and post-office address of the district officers elect, within two weeks after the said officers shall have been elected or appointed and qualified. The clerk shall also report to the county superintendent the time of the commencement of each term of school, within two weeks from the commencement of such term.

Report of Indebtedness.—SEC. 55. [Laws 1877, Ch. 90, Sec. 1.] That in addition to the duties now required by law of the following officers, to wit, township clerks, and clerks of incorporated cities, school-district clerks, and clerks of boards of education, they shall each of them make and transmit to the clerk of their respective counties, on or before the 5th day of July in each year, a complete certified statement of the floating and bonded indebtedness, with date of issuing and of maturing of outstanding bonds, amount of sinking fund, if any, for redeeming the same, and such other information as may be required by the county clerks concerning the financial condition of their respective townships, cities or districts; and when no outstanding indebtedness exists, such fact shall be reported.

Records.—SEC. 56. [Laws 1876, Ch. 122, Art. 4, Sec. 20.] Every school-district clerk or treasurer who shall neglect or refuse to deliver to his successor in office all records, books and papers belonging to his office, shall be subject to a fine not exceeding fifty dollars.

Treasurer; Bond.—SEC. 57. [Laws 1879, Ch. 156, Sec. 1.] The treasurer shall execute to the district a bond in double the amount, as near as can be ascertained, to come into his hands as treasurer during the year, with sufficient securities, to be approved by the director and clerk, conditioned to the faithful discharge of the duties of said office. Such bond shall be justified by the affidavit of the principal and his sureties: *Provided,* That the director of the district or the county superintendent of public instruction shall be authorized to administer the oaths in the justification of the treasurer and his sureties. And said bond shall be filed with the district clerk, and in case of the breach of any condition thereof, the director shall cause a suit to be commenced thereon, in the name of the district, and the money collected shall be applied by such director to the use of the district, as the same should have been applied by the treasurer; and if such director shall neglect or refuse to prosecute, then any householder in the district may cause such prosecution to be instituted.

Duties.—SEC. 58. [Laws 1876, Ch. 122, Art. 4, Sec. 15.] The treasurer of each district shall pay out, on the order of the clerk, signed by the director of the district, all public moneys which shall come into his hands for the use of the district.

Receive School Moneys.—SEC. 59. [Laws 1876, Ch. 122, Art. 4, Sec. 16.] The county treasurer shall pay to each district treasurer in the county all school moneys in the county treasury belonging to the district, upon the order of the director and clerk of the district: *Provided,* That said order shall be accompanied by a certificate from the district clerk stating that the treasurer of the district has executed and filed his bond as required by law.

District Taxes.—SEC. 60. [Laws 1876, Ch. 122, Art. 4, Sec. 17.] Where a school-district tax has been voted, and from the fault or negligence of any officer or any other cause has not been levied and collected

---

SEC. 57. It is not proper for either the director or the clerk to become surety for the treasurer. The bond should be executed before the treasurer is sworn. The bond becoming insufficient from any cause, the director and clerk may require the bond to be made good.

in any year, the same shall be added to and collected with the taxes of
the year following; and the county treasurer shall pay over to the treasurers of the respective school districts all taxes he may have collected
for the said districts, on the order of the district clerk, countersigned
by the director, subject to the proviso contained in section fifty-two
[sec. 57, art. 4] of this act.

Records and Reports.—SEC. 61. [Laws 1876, Ch. 122, Art. 4,
Sec. 18.] The treasurer shall keep a book in which he shall enter all the
moneys received and disbursed by him, specifying particularly the sources
from which money has been received, and the person or persons to whom
and the objects for which the same has been paid out. He shall present
to the district at each annual meeting a report in writing, containing a
statement of all moneys received by him from the county treasurer during the year; also all moneys collected by him during the year from
assessments in the district, and of the disbursements made by him, with
the items of such disbursements, and exhibit the vouchers therefor, which
report shall be recorded by the district clerk; and at the close of his
term of office shall settle with the district board, and shall hand over to
his successor said book, and all receipts, vouchers, orders and papers
coming into his hands as treasurer of the district, together with all the
moneys remaining in his hands as such treasurer.

Prosecution.—SEC. 62. [Laws 1876, Ch. 122, Art. 4, Sec. 19.] If
any district treasurer shall refuse or neglect to pay over any money in
his hands belonging to the district, it shall be the duty of his successor
in office to prosecute, without delay, the official bond of such treasurer
for the recovery of such money.

School House.—SEC. 63. [Laws 1876, Ch. 122, Art. 4, Sec. 21.]
The district board shall purchase or lease such a site for a school house
as shall have been designated by the voters at a district meeting, in the
corporate name thereof, and shall build, hire or purchase such school
house as the voters of the district in a district meeting shall have agreed
upon, out of the funds provided for that purpose, and make sale of any
school-house site or other property of the district, and if necessary, execute a conveyance of the same in the name of their office, when lawfully
directed by the voters of such district at any regular or special meeting,
and shall carry into effect all lawful orders of the district.

School Property.—SEC. 64. [Laws 1876, Ch. 122, Art. 4, Sec. 22.]
The district board shall have the care and keeping of the school house,
and other property belonging to the district. They shall have power to
make such rules and regulations relating to the district library as they
may deem proper, and to appoint some suitable person to act as librarian, and to take charge of the school apparatus belonging to the district.

Non-resident Pupils.—SEC. 65. [Laws 1876, Ch. 122, Art. 4, Sec. 23.] The district board shall have power to admit scholars from adjoining districts.

Teachers.—SEC. 66. [Laws 1876, Ch. 122, Art. 4, Sec. 24.] The district board in each district' shall contract with and hire qualified teachers for and in the name of the district, which contract shall be in writing, and shall specify the wages per week or month as agreed upon by the parties, and such contract shall be filed in the district clerk's office; and, in conjunction with the county superintendent, may dismiss for incompetency, cruelty, negligence, or immorality.

Necessary Appendages.—SEC. 67. [Laws 1876, Ch. 122, Art. 4, Sec. 25.] The district board shall provide the necessary appendages for the school house during the time a school is taught therein, and shall keep an accurate account of all expenses thus incurred, and present the same for allowance at any regular district meeting.

Suspend Pupil; Appeal.—SEC. 68. [Laws 1876, Ch. 122, Art. 4, Sec. 26.] The district board may suspend, or authorize the director to suspend, from the privileges of a school, any pupil guilty of immorality or persistent violation of the regulations of the school, which suspension shall not extend beyond the current quarter of the school: *Provided,* That the pupil suspended shall have the right to appeal from the decision of said board of directors to the county superintendent, who shall, upon a full investigation of the charges preferred against said pupil, determine as to his guilt or innocence of the offense charged, whose decision shall be final.

School Duties —SEC. 69. [Laws 1876, Ch. 122, Art. 4, Sec. 27.] The district board shall furnish each teacher with a suitable daily register, and shall visit together, or by one or two of their number, all the schools of their district, at least once a term, and at such other periods during the term as in their opinion the exigencies of each school may require; at which visits they shall examine the register of the teacher and see that it is properly kept, and inquire into other matters touching

---

SEC. 66. (*a*) In view of this section, read in connection with section 94, which makes it the duty of the county board of examiners to examine *all persons proposing to teach in the common schools of the county,* it is held (1) that a "qualified" teacher is one holding a legal certificate in force at the time of opening school, and (2) that a school taught by a person not holding such certificate is not, within the meaning of the law, a "common school." As the "*qualification*" of a teacher begins at the date of issue, and ends at the date of expiration, of the certificate which confers the qualification, it is the duty of the district board to see to it that a teacher in their employ, whose certificate expires during school term, shall, at the risk of dismissal upon the expiration of said certicate, preserve the status of a "*qualified*" teacher in the only way allowable by law, *i. e.*, by procuring, in season, a *new* certificate by "*passing*" at a public examination lawfully held.

(*b*) The district board cannot legally contract with or hire a qualified teacher who is a member of the board. A contract made by a district board with one of their own number, being contrary to public policy, is held to be null and void.

(*c*) A district board cannot dismiss a teacher without the concurrence of the county superintendent.

the school house, facilities for ventilation, furniture, apparatus, library, studies, discipline, modes of teaching, and improvement of the school; shall confer with the teacher in regard to condition and management, and make such suggestions as in their view would promote the interest and efficiency of the school, and the progress and good order of the pupils. The date and results of such visits shall be entered by the clerk of the board on their minutes.

Uniformity of Text-Books.—SEC. 70. [Laws 1879, Ch. 157, Sec. 1.] The district board, each board of education, and each and every school-district board, shall require a uniform series of text-books to be used in each separate branch of study in each school; but each board shall determine for itself, within six months from the passage of this act, the particular series of text-books which shall be used, and when such selection of text-books shall hereafter be adopted and introduced in pursuance of the provisions of this act by said boards, no change shall be made for a period of five years from the date of such introduction of any particular series of text-books, unless four-fifths of the legal voters of any such district shall petition for a change in the series of text-books adopted; but no member of the said boards, or either of them, nor any teacher, while employed as such teacher, shall act as agent for any author, publisher or bookseller, nor shall any member of the said boards, or either or any one of them, or any employed teacher, directly or indirectly receive any gift, emolument or reward for his or her influence in recommending or introducing any book, school apparatus or furniture of any kind whatever.

Penalty.—SEC. 71. [Laws 1879, Ch. 157, Sec. 2.] That any member of any school-district board or board of education who shall violate any of the provisions of this act shall be deemed guilty of a misdemeanor, and on conviction shall be punished by a fine not less than twenty-five dollars nor more than one hundred dollars, or by imprisonment in the county jail for a period not less than six months, or by both such fine and imprisonment; and any teacher who shall violate any of the provisions of this act shall be liable to immediate dismissal.

Disposition of Fines.—SEC. 72. [Laws 1879, Ch. 157, Sec. 3.] All fines collected for any violation of this act shall be paid to the treasurer of the county where the suit is brought, for the support of common schools.

Taxes.—SEC. 73. [Laws 1876, Ch. 122, Art. 4, Sec. 30.] It shall be the duty of the school-district boards of the various school districts in the respective counties of the state to cause to be certified by the school-district clerk to the county clerk of their respective counties, on or before the 25th day of August, annually, the aggregate percentage by them levied on the real and personal property in each district, as returned on the assessment roll of the county; and the county clerk is hereby authorized and required to place the same on the tax roll of said county, in a separate column or columns, designating the purpose for which such taxes were levied; and the said taxes shall be collected by the county treasurer and paid over to the treasurers of the respective school districts in the county, with the same power and restrictions and under the same regulations, and in all respects, as to the sale of real or personal property. He shall be authorized, and he is hereby required, to act according to the provisions and requisitions of the law for the collection of the taxes for state and county purposes.

Judgments.—SEC. 74. [Laws 1876, Ch. 122, Art. 4, Sec. 31.] Whenever any final judgment shall be obtained against any school district, the district board shall levy a tax on such taxable property in the district for the payment thereof. Such tax shall be collected as other school-district taxes, but no execution shall issue on such judgment against the school district; and in case the district board neglect to levy a tax as aforesaid, for the space of thirty days after such judgment shall become final, or in case the proper officer shall neglect to collect the tax levied within the time and in the manner provided by law, then the judgment creditor of the district may have and recover a judgment against the officer or officers so in default, for the amount due him on such judgment against the district, with costs, upon which execution shall issue.

Removal of School Houses, etc.—SEC. 75. [Laws 1876, Ch. 122, Art. 4, Sec. 32.] That whenever a school house or other improvements have been made upon the claim of any settler upon any of the public, Indian or railroad lands within this state, to which the said settler had no title, it shall be lawful for the school directors of the proper school district to remove the said school house or other improvements from the said claim at any time within one year from the time that the settler in any given case may acquire a title to his said claim: *Provided,* That if the said settler, in any given case, shall convey to said board of school directors one acre of the land upon which said school house or other improvements are situated, the same shall not be removed: *And provided further,* That if any school house shall have been built of stone, brick or frame, costing not less than five hundred dollars, the probate judge of the county shall appoint three disinterested persons, who shall appraise and condemn one acre of such land upon which said improvements shall have been located; and it shall be the duty of the school directors of such district to pay to the owner of such land the value of such land as found by said appraisers.

Use of School House.—SEC. 76. [Laws 1876, Ch. 125, Sec. 1.] The district board shall have the care and keeping of the school house and other property belonging to the district. They are hereby authorized to open the school house for the use of religious, political, literary, scientific, mechanical or agricultural societies belonging to their district, for the purpose of holding the business of public meetings of said societies, under such regulations as the school board may adopt.

ARTICLE V.—DISTRICT SCHOOLS.

§77. Branches taught in public schools; instruction shall be given in the English branches.
78. School month defined.
79. District schools free to all resident children.

§80. Penalty for violation of this article; shall not apply to officers of cities of first and second class.
81. Pupils with contagious diseases excluded, when.
82. When a tuition fee may be assessed.

Branches Taught.—SEC. 77. [Laws 1877, Ch. 170, Sec. 1.] That in each and every school district shall be taught orthography, reading, writing, English grammar, geography and arithmetic, and such other branches as may be determined by the district board: *Provided*, That the instruction given in the several branches taught shall be in the English language.

School Month.—SEC. 78. [Laws 1876, Ch. 122, Art. 5, Sec. 2.] A school month shall consist of four weeks of five days each of six hours per day.

Free Schools.—SEC. 79. [Laws 1876, Ch. 122, Art. 5, Sec. 3.] The district schools established under the provisions of this act shall at all times be equally free and accessible to all the children resident therein over five and under the age of twenty-one years, subject to such regulations as the district board in each may prescribe.

Penalty.—SEC. 80. [Laws 1877, Ch. 170, Sec. 2.] The members of any district board willfully violating any of the provisions of this article, or refusing the admission of any children into the common schools, shall forfeit to the county the sum of one hundred dollars each for every month so offending during which such schools are taught; and all moneys forfeited to the common-school fund of the county under this act, shall be expended by the county superintendent for the education of such children in the school district thus denied equal educational advantages: *Provided*, That any member of said board who shall protest against the action of his said board in excluding any children from

---

SEC. 80. The words "any children," used in the opening sentence and in the proviso of this section, must obviously mean any children *of school age residing in the district.* Section 65 authorizes but does not require the district board to admit scholars from *adjoining districts.*

equal educational advantages, or in violating any of the provisions of this article, shall not be subject to the penalty herein named: *And provided further*, That the provisions of this act shall not apply to cities of the first or second class.

Contagious Disease.—SEC. 81. [Laws 1876, Ch. 122, Art. 5, Sec. 5.] No pupil infected with any contagious disease shall be allowed to attend any common school or remain in any school room while so infected.

Tuition Fee.—SEC. 82. [Laws 1876, Ch. 122, Art. 5, Sec. 6.] Whenever there be not public money enough belonging to any school district to support a public school the length of time determined at the annual meeting, or at a special meeting duly called, the district board, to meet said deficiency, may assess a tuition fee upon each scholar attending said school, the assessment to be proportioned to the number of days each pupil has been in actual attendance during the term: *Provided*, That no tuition fee shall be levied upon the scholars in any of the public schools of this state, in accordance with the provisions of this act, unless the entire amount of one per cent. for teachers' wages, as required by law, be first assessed upon the taxable property of said school district.

ARTICLE VI.—TEACHERS, NORMAL INSTITUTES, AND CERTIFICATES.

83. Teachers shall keep a record of attendance, deportment and recitations; report to district clerk.

84. Normal institutes to be held annually.

85. Conductors and instructors; certificate of special qualifications required.

86. Normal institute fund, how raised; each candidate for a teacher's certificate shall pay a fee of one dollar.

87. County treasurer, custodian of fund.

88. County superintendent shall transmit funds to county treasurer.

89. State superintendent of public instruction shall certify to state auditor the number of persons enrolled in each institute; auditor shall issue order on state treasurer for fifty dollars.

90. Institute fund, how disbursed.

91. County superintendent shall execute bond.

92. Union institutes, how formed; custodian of fund.

93. County board of examiners, how constituted; qualifications and appointment of examiners.

94. Public examinations; notice of same.

95. Grades of certificates.

96. First grade, to whom issued.

97. Second grade, to whom issued.

98. Third grade, to whom issued; limitation upon issue of same; standings required for each grade.

99. County certificates of force, where; may be revoked, for what causes.

100. State board of education, how constituted; may issue state diplomas, to whom; may issue state certificates, to whom; shall meet where, and how often.

Records and Reports.—SEC. 83. [Laws 1876, Ch. 122, Art. 6, Sec. 1.] It shall be the duty of the teachers of every district school or graded school to keep, in a register for this purpose, a daily record of the attendance and the deportment of each pupil, and of the recitation of each pupil in the several branches pursued in said school, and to make out and file with the district clerk, at the expiration of each term of the school, a full report of the whole number of scholars admitted to school during such term, distinguishing between male and female, the text-books used, the branches taught, and the number of pupils engaged in the study of said branches, and any other information the district board or county superintendent may require. The wages of a teacher for the last month of a school term shall not be paid by any district board, unless said teacher shall have complied with the requirements of this section.

Normal Institutes.—SEC. 84. [Laws 1877, Ch. 136, Sec. 1.] The county superintendents of·public instruction shall hold annually, in their respective counties, for a term of not less than four weeks, a normal institute for the instruction of teachers and those desiring to teach: *Provided*, That in the sparsely-settled portions of the state, two or more counties may be united in holding one normal institute, as hereinafter provided.

Conductor and Instructors.—SEC. 85. [Laws 1877, Ch. 136, Sec. 2.] The county superintendent of public instruction, with the advice and consent of the state superintendent of public instruction, shall determine the time and place of holding such normal institutes, and shall select a conductor and instructors for the same: *Provided*, That no person shall be paid from the institute funds for services as conductor or instructor of said institutes who has not received a certificate from the state board of examiners as to his special qualifications for that work.

Normal-Institute Fund.—SEC. 86. [Laws 1877, Ch. 136, Sec. 3.] To defray the expenses of said institute, the county superintendent shall require the payment of a fee of one dollar from each candidate for a teacher's certificate, and the payment of one dollar registration fee for each person attending the normal institute; and the board of county commissioners may appropriate, as may by them be deemed necessary, for the further support of such institutes: *Provided*, Such appropriation does not, in any one year, exceed the sum of one hundred dollars.

Custodian.—Sec. 87. [Laws 1877, Ch. 136, Sec. 4.] The fund thus created shall be designated the "normal-institute fund," and the county treasurer shall be the custodian of the said fund.

Monthly Reports.—SEC. 88. [Laws 1877, Ch. 136, Sec. 5.] The county superintendent shall, monthly, and at the close of each institute, transmit to the county treasurer all moneys received by him, as provided in section three, together with the name of each person so contributing, and the amount; and the county treasurer shall place all such moneys to the credit of the "normal-institute fund."

SEC. 86. The county superintendent must require the payment of a fee of one dollar from each *candidate* for a teacher's certificate. This fee should be collected in advance, and it cannot be returned to the unsuccessful applicant.

State Aid.—SEC. 89. [Laws 1877, Ch. 136, Sec. 6.] It shall be the duty of the state superintendent of public instruction, annually, when fifty persons have registered as members of any normal institute organized under the provisions of this act, and have paid the required registration fee, to certify the same to the auditor of state, who shall forward to the county treasurer of said county an order on the treasurer of the state for the sum of fifty dollars, to be paid out of any money appropriated for that purpose; which amount the county treasurer shall place to the credit of the "normal-institute fund." And the sum of three thousand dollars, or so much thereof as may be required, is hereby appropriated for the purposes herein named for the fiscal year ending June 30, 1878, and the same amount for the fiscal year ending June 30, 1879.

Disbursements.—SEC. 90. [Laws 1877, Ch. 136, Sec. 7.] All disbursements of the "normal-institute fund" shall be upon the order of the county superintendent, and no orders shall be drawn on said fund except for claims, approved by the county superintendent, for services rendered or expenses incurred in connection with the normal institutes.

Bond.—SEC. 91. [Laws 1877, Ch. 136, Sec. 8.] Each county superintendent of public instruction shall, immediately after the passage of this act, and hereafter, before entering upon the duties of his office, execute a bond to the state of Kansas in the sum of one thousand dollars, with one or more sureties, conditioned for the faithful performance of his duties, which bond shall be approved by the county clerk, and filed in his office.

Union Institutes.—SEC. 92. [Laws 1877, Ch. 136, Sec. 9.] Two or more counties, each having less than three thousand inhabitants, may be united in holding one normal institute, with the consent and by the direction of the state superintendent of public instruction: *Provided,* That the several county superintendents of the counties thus uniting shall choose one of their number to act for them in determining the time and place of holding the normal institute, and in selecting a conductor and instructors for the same, as provided in section 2: *And provided,* That the person thus chosen shall draw all orders upon the "normal-institute fund," as provided in section 7 [90]: *And provided,* That the treasurer of the county in which such normal institute is held shall be the custodian of the "normal-institute fund," to whom the state and county appropriations for the benefit of the normal institute shall be transmitted, and to whom the several county superintendents of the counties thus uniting shall transmit the fees collected as provided in section 3 [86].

SEC. 90. See also section 85. It is unlawful for the county treasurer to pay an order on the normal-institute fund drawn "for services rendered," in favor of any person not holding the certificate of the state board of education, for institute work.

3

County Board of Examiners.—SEC. 93. [Laws 1881, Ch. 151, Sec. 1.] In each county there shall be a county board of examiners, composed of the county superintendent, who shall be *ex-officio* chairman of the board, and two competent persons, holders of first-grade certificates, to be appointed by the county commissioners on the nomination of the county superintendent, who shall serve one year from the time of their respective appointments, and receive for their services the sum of three dollars per day for not to exceed three days in any one quarter of a year.

Public Examinations.—SEC. 94. [Laws 1881, Ch. 151, Sec. 2.] The board, two of whom shall constitute a quorum, shall publicly examine at such times and places as may be designated by the chairman, who shall give ten days' notice of each of such examinations, all persons proposing to teach in the common schools of the county, (cities of the first and second class excepted,) as to their competency to teach the branches prescribed by law; and such board of examiners shall issue certificates as hereinafter provided, to all such applicants as shall pass the requisite examination, and satisfy the board as to their good moral character and their ability to teach and govern school successfully.

Grades of Certificates.—SEC. 95. [Laws 1881, Ch. 151, Sec. 3.] Certificates issued by county boards shall be of three grades—first, second and third—and shall continue in force respectively two years, one year, and six months.

First Grade, to Whom Issued.—SEC. 96. [Laws 1881, Ch. 151, Sec. 4.] Certificates of the first grade shall continue in force for two years, and shall certify that the person to whom issued is proficient in, and fully qualified to teach, orthography, reading, writing, English grammar and composition, geography, arithmetic, United States history, constitution of the United States, book-keeping, physiology, elements of natural philosophy. And they shall not be issued to persons under eighteen years of age, nor to such as have not taught successfully twelve months.

SEC. 93. (*a*) Examiners appointed after March 9, 1881, must be "holders of first-grade certificates," granted under the existing law. Holders of state or A-grade certificates are not, in virtue thereof, eligible to be examiners.

(*b*) Until appointments are made in accordance with the new law, the old members hold over.

(*c*) County superintendents are not required, as members of the board of examiners, to be holders of first-grade certificates.

SEC. 94. (*a*) An examination is not "public" unless every one who desires to do so is permitted to know the questions put to and the answers returned by the candidates for certificates. In oral examinations, of course it is every person's privilege to hear all that is said by both examiner and applicant. In written examinations, it would be well to have all papers submitted by the candidates filed in the office of the county superintendent, where interested parties could see them at any time. If this were done, it would compel examiners to be impartial in their grading, often relieving them from very unjust criticism; and it would greatly assist school officers in making selections of teachers.

(*b*) Should an examiner desire to "pass" at a public examination, conducted by the two other members of the board, his examination should certainly be thorough and exhaustive. The county superintendent cannot legally examine one of the members of the board and issue to him a certificate, without the assistance and concurrence of the other member of the board

Second Grade, to Whom Issued.—SEC. 97. [Laws 1881, Ch. 151, Sec. 5.] Certificates of the second grade may be issued to persons of not less than seventeen years of age, who have taught successfully not less than three months, and who shall fully satisfy the board as to their ability to teach all the branches prescribed for first-grade certificates, except physiology, book-keeping and elements of natural philosophy.

Third Grade, to Whom Issued; Provisos.—SEC. 98. [Laws 1881, Ch. 151, Sec. 6.] Third-grade certificates may be issued to persons not less than sixteen years of age, who are proficient in orthography, reading, writing, English grammar, geography, arithmetic, and United States history; but in no case shall a third-grade certificate be given a second time to the same person: *Provided further,* 1st. That persons who receive a first-grade certificate shall make a general average of not less than 90 per cent., and in no case shall a person receive a certificate of first-grade who does not make at least 70 per cent. in any one branch. 2d. Persons who receive a second-grade certificate shall make a general average of not less than 80 per cent., and in no case shall any person receive a certificate of second grade who makes less than 60 per cent. in any one branch. 3d. Persons who receive a third-grade certificate shall make a general average of not less than 70 per cent., and in no case shall any person receive a third-grade certificate who makes less than 60 per cent. in any one branch.

(e) The awarding of a certificate, or any other act within the jurisdiction of the board, must have duly received, in the lawful course of business, the consent of at least two members of the board, in order to be, legally, an act *of the board.* County certificates can be legally granted only by *the board.*

(d) The county superintendent, as chairman of the board, may designate times and places of examinations.

(e) A county certificate cannot be lawfully dated back beyond the time when the county board, in the lawful course of business, actually awarded the same.

(f) Although county boards may, by revocation for cause, abridge, they cannot lawfully extend, the time during which a certificate issued by them shall be in force, nor renew the same without a public examination of the holder thereof.

SEC. 96. This experience need not have been had in Kansas, but must be shown to the satisfaction of the board of examiners.

SEC. 98. (a) No certificate of the third grade can be issued a second time to the same person in a given county, but there is nothing in the law which can be construed to restrict a person from obtaining one third-grade certificate in each county in the state; but a second one would be void and of no force. In the case of applicants who have never taught, I recommend examining boards to issue *Statements of Standing*, certifying that the holders are entitled to have a third-grade certificate issued to them on call, to expire six months from date of statement. Such papers will satisfy school boards that the parties are legally-qualified teachers; and, on the other hand, such teachers, in failing to make engagements, are not barred from another trial in the county. The object of the law is to compel improvement among teachers; and the only hardship that could arise by its operation is the one for which this remedy is suggested.

(b) A full single public examination is the only legal basis for the issue of a certificate. It is the province of the board to determine the standing of the applicant in every study; if that standing is in every particular what this section requires, the certificate *may be issued;* but the board should inquire into the "competency" of the candidate to teach and govern a school successfully. This competency is not to be assumed from the fact that the applicant passes the examination; it must be shown to the satisfaction of the examiners.

Certificates, of Force Where; Revocation.—SEC. 99. [Laws 1881, Ch. 151, Sec. 7.]

No certificate shall be of force, except in the county in which it is issued. The certificates issued under this act may be revoked by the board of examiners on the ground of immorality, or for any cause which would have justified the withholding thereof when the same was granted.

State Board of Education; Diplomas.—SEC. 100. [Laws 1876, Ch. 122, Art. 6, Sec. 7.]

There shall be a state board of education, consisting of the state superintendent of public instruction, the chancellor of the state university, the president of the state agricultural college, and the principals of the state normal schools at Emporia and Leavenworth. The state board of education thus constituted are hereby authorized and empowered to issue state diplomas to such professional teachers as may be found, upon a critical examination, to possess the requisite scholarship and culture, and who may also exhibit satisfactory evidence of an unexceptionable moral character, and of eminent professional experience and ability, and who have taught for two years in the state. All such diplomas shall be countersigned by the state superintendent of public instruction, and shall supersede the necessity of any and all other examinations of the person holding the same by county, city or local boards of examiners; and such diplomas shall be valid in any county, city, town or school district in the state during the lifetime of the holder, unless revoked by the state board of education.

State Certificates.—SEC. 101. [Laws 1876, Ch. 122, Art. 6, Sec. 8.]

The state board of education are furthermore authorized and empowered to issue state certificates of high qualifications to such teachers as may be found, upon examination, to possess the requisite scholarship, and who may also exhibit satisfactory evidence of good moral character, and ability to teach, and skill to govern and control children. The certificates issued by the state board of education may be of two grades— one for three years and one for five years; and all certificates issued by said board shall be countersigned by the state superintendent of public instruction, and such state certificates shall supersede the necessity of all other examinations of the persons holding them by county or local

---

It is proper for the board to refuse especially the first-grade or second-grade certificate to applicants passing the necessary examination but not satisfying the board of their ability to "teach and govern school successfully." Applicants are examined *as to their competency to teach* (see section 94); and while they may be ninety or ninety-nine on examination, they are not necessarily possessed of such "ability to teach" (see sec. 97) as will justify the issuing of the best certificate. I hope the time will soon come (and be hastened in its coming by the action of examiners) when it cannot be truthfully said that there are better teachers holding the second grade than there are holding the first grade.

SEC. 99. County certificates issued in county A cannot be legally made valid in county B, even by the indorsement of the board of examiners of county B; for the law expressly provides that "no [county] certificate shall be of force except in the county in which it is issued."

boards of examiners; and such certificate shall be valid in any county, city, town or school district in the state for the term of three or five years (as therein set forth), unless sooner revoked by said state board of education.

State Examinations.—SEC. 102. [Laws 1876, Ch. 122, Art. 6, Sec. 9.] The state board of education shall meet at the city of Topeka on the fourth Monday of August in each year, and at such other times and places as may by them be deemed necessary, and proceed to the transaction of such business as may legally come before them, and to examine all applicants who may present themselves for such examination; and if satisfied with the scholarship, culture, and moral character of the applicant, and with his professional attainments and experience, said board shall issue a state diploma, or certificate, as the case may be, in accordance with such examinations and the provisions of this act: *Provided,* That the provisions of this act shall be carried out without expense to the state.

ARTICLE VII.—UNION OR GRADED–SCHOOL DISTRICTS.

How Formed.—SEC. 103. [Laws 1876, Ch. 122, Art. 7, Sec. 1.] Whenever the inhabitants of two or more school districts may wish to unite for the purpose of establishing a graded school in which instruction shall be given in the higher branches of education, the clerks of the several districts shall, upon a written application of five voters of the respective districts, call a meeting of the voters of such districts, at some convenient place, by posting up written notices thereof, in like manner as provided for calling district meetings; and if a majority of the voters of each of the two or more districts shall vote to unite for the purpose herein stated, they shall, at that meeting or at an adjourned meeting, elect a board of directors, consisting of a director, clerk and treasurer.

Duties of Board.—SEC. 104. [Laws 1876, Ch. 122, Art. 7, Sec. 2.] The board of directors provided in the preceding section shall, in all matters relating to the graded schools, possess all the powers and discharge all the like duties of the district board of directors, as prescribed in this act.

School Funds.—Sec. 105. [Laws 1876, Ch. 122, Art. 7, Sec. 3.] The union district thus formed shall be entitled to an equitable share of the school funds, to be drawn from the treasurer of each district so uniting, in proportion to the number of children attending the said graded school for each district.

Levy Taxes.—Sec. 106. [Laws 1876, Ch. 122, Art. 7, Sec. 4.] The said union district may levy taxes for the purpose of purchasing a building or furnishing proper buildings for the accommodation of the school or for the purpose of defraying necessary expenses and paying teachers, but shall be governed in all respects by the law herein provided for levying and collecting district taxes.

Apportionment.—Sec. 107. [Laws 1876, Ch. 122, Art. 7, Sec. 5.] The clerk of the union district shall report in writing to the treasurer of each school district uniting in the union district, the number of scholars attending the graded school from his district, their sex, and the branches studied; and the said district treasurer shall apportion the amount of school money due the union district, and pay the same over to the treasurer of the union district on order of the clerk and director thereof.

Clerk.—Sec. 108. [Laws 1876, Ch. 122, Art. 7, Sec. 6.] The clerk of the union district shall make a report to the county superintendent of public instruction, and discharge all the duties of clerk in like manner as clerk of the district.

Treasurer.—Sec. 109. [Laws 1876, Ch. 122, Art. 7, Sec. 7.] The treasurer of the union district shall perform all the duties of treasurer as prescribed in this act, in like manner as the district treasurer.

Apportionment to Cities.—Sec. 110. [Laws 1876, Ch. 122, Art. 7, Sec. 8.] The public schools of any city, town or village, which may be regulated by special law set forth in the charter of such city, town or village, shall be entitled to receive their proportion of the public school fund: *Provided,* The clerk of the board of education in such city, town or village shall make due report within the time and manner prescribed in this act, to the county superintendent of public instruction.

Single District.—Sec. 111. [Laws 1876, Ch. 122, Art. 7, Sec. 9.] Any single district shall possess power to establish graded schools, subject to the provisions of this article, in like manner as two or more districts united.

Annual Meeting.—Sec. 112. [Laws 1876, Ch. 122, Art. 7, Sec. 10.] The annual meeting of union or graded-school districts shall be held on the last Wednesday in June, at such hour as may be indicated by the board.

ARTICLE VIII.—School-District Libraries.

Library Fund.—Section 113. [Laws 1876, Ch. 122, Art. 8, Sec. 1.] That the several school districts of the state may, at the annual meeting in each year, vote a tax upon all the taxable property of the district, not to exceed two mills on the dollar, which tax shall be certified by the district clerk to the county clerk, at the same time and manner as other school-district taxes are certified; and the county clerk shall place the same on the tax roll of the county in a separate column, designating the purpose for which such tax was levied; and said tax shall be collected and paid over to the treasurer of said district in all respects as other school-district taxes are collected and paid: *Provided, however*, That in the districts where the taxable property of the district is more than twenty thousand dollars and not more than thirty thousand, there shall not be levied more than one and a half mills on the dollar; and where the taxable property is more than thirty thousand dollars and not more than fifty thousand, there shall not be levied more than one mill on the dollar; and in all cases where the taxable property of the district shall exceed fifty thousand dollars, there shall not be levied more than one half-mill on the dollar.

How Used.—Sec. 114. [Laws 1876, Ch. 122, Art. 8, Sec. 2.] The money so collected shall be used under the direction of the board of directors, for the purchasing of a school-district library, and for no other purpose; and the district board, in the purchase of books, shall be confined to works of history, biography, science and travels.

Librarian; Rules.—Sec. 115. [Laws 1876, Ch. 122, Art. 8, Sec. 3.] The district clerk shall be the librarian, unless the board of directors shall appoint some other competent and suitable person, who shall reside in the district, to perform the duties of that office; and the board shall have power to make such rules and regulations in regard to the management of said library as they shall deem best, and they shall revise and change said rules from time to time as the necessities of the case may require.

ARTICLE IX.—Fines and Penalties.

Jurisdiction.—Sec. 116. [Laws 1876, Ch. 122, Art. 9, Sec. 1.] Justices of the peace shall have jurisdiction in all cases in which a school district is a party interested, when the amount claimed by the plaintiff shall not exceed one hundred dollars; and the parties shall have the right of appeal, as in other cases.

How Collected.—SEC. 117. [Laws 1876, Ch. 122, Art. 9, Sec. 2.] All fines and penalties not otherwise provided for in this act shall be collected by an action in any court of competent jurisdiction.

Penalty for Receiving Bonus.—SEC. 118. [Laws 1876, Ch. 122, Art. 9, Sec. 3.] If the state superintendent, or any county superintendent of public instruction, shall receive from the publisher of any school books, or from any other person interested in the sale or introduction of any book into the public schools in the state, any money or bonus in any manner as an inducement for the recommendation or introduction of any such book into the public schools of the state, such superintendent shall, upon conviction thereof before any court of competent jurisdiction, be found guilty of a misdemeanor, and shall be fined in a sum not less than one thousand dollars nor exceeding five thousand dollars, or shall be imprisoned in the penitentiary for any time not less than one year nor more than five years, or both such fine and imprisonment.

ARTICLE X.—PUBLIC SCHOOLS IN CITIES OF THE FIRST CLASS.

Defined.—SEC. 119. [Laws 1876, Ch. 122, Art. 10, Sec. 1.] All cities of more than fifteen thousand inhabitants shall be governed by the provisions of this act.

Board of Education.—SEC. 120. [Laws 1881, Ch. 149, Sec. 2.] In each city under this act there shall be a board of education, consisting of three members from each ward, (who shall be and remain residents of the ward for which they are elected during their term of office,) to be elected by the qualified voters at large of the said city, one of whom in each ward shall be elected annually, and shall hold his office for the term of three years and until his successor shall be elected and qualified: *Provided,* That this amendment shall not affect nor change the terms of office of the several members of the board of education of cities of the first class now in office: *And provided further,* That in any city of the second class hereafter organized as a city of the first class, the terms of office of any member of the board of education which would expire prior to the first Monday of August after such organization, is hereby extended to the said first Monday of August.

Vacancy in Board.—SEC. 121. [Laws 1876, Ch. 122, Art. 10, Sec. 3.] The board of education shall have power to fill any vacancy which may occur in their body: *Provided,* That any vacancy occurring more than ten days previous to the annual city election, and leaving an unexpired term of one or more years, shall be filled at the first city election thereafter; and the ballots and returns of election shall be designated as follows: "To fill unexpired term of —— years."

Powers of Board.—SEC. 122. [Laws 1876, Ch. 122, Art. 10, Sec. 4.] The board of education shall have power to select their own officers; to make their rules and regulations, subject to the provisions of this act; to establish a high school, whenever in their opinion the educational interests of the city demand the same; and to exercise the sole control over the public schools and school property of the city.

Organization; Annual Reports.—SEC. 123. [Laws 1876, Ch. 122, Art. 10, Sec. 5.] The board of education shall at its first regular meeting in August organize by the election of a president and vice president from its own members, each of whom shall serve for one year, and until his successor is elected and qualified. They may elect a clerk, who shall hold his office during the pleasure of the board; and may elect a superintendent of public schools, who shall not be a member of the board, and who shall hold his office during the pleasure of the board. The fiscal year of such board shall close on the last day of June, and the annual reports of the president, superintendent, and of the several committees, shall be presented to the board on or before the first Monday in August in each year; and the term of office of the president and vice president of the year eighteen hundred and seventy-one, and of the several members of the board now in office, is extended so that their several terms of office shall expire on the first Monday of August instead of the first Monday of May.

President.—SEC. 124. [Laws 1876, Ch. 122, Art. 10, Sec. 6.] It shall be the duty of the president to preside at all meetings of the board of education, to appoint all committees whose appointment is not otherwise provided for, and to sign all warrants ordered by the board of education to be drawn upon the city treasurer for school moneys.

Vice President.—SEC. 125. [Laws 1876, Ch. 122, Art. 10, Sec. 7.] It shall be the duty of the vice president to perform all the duties of the president, in case of his absence or disability.

Clerk; Superintendent.—SEC. 126. [Laws 1876, Ch. 122, Art. 10, Sec. 8.] It shall be the duty of the clerk to attend all meetings of the board, to keep an accurate journal of its proceedings, to have the care and custody of the records and papers of the board, to countersign all warrants drawn upon the treasurer by order of the board, to keep an account of all moneys paid to the treasurer on account of said board, and of all moneys paid or orders drawn on the treasurer by order of said board; and shall, at least once in every three months, prepare and cause to be published in said city a statement, under oath, showing— 1st. The moneys received by the treasurer since last report, and from what source received; 2d. The amount of sinking fund, and how invested; 3d. The moneys paid out, to whom, and for what paid; 4th. The balance of general fund in the hands of the treasurer; 5th. The number, date and amount of any bond issued by said board, purchased under the authority in this act given, and the amount paid therefor; and shall perform such other duties as the board or its committees may require, and shall receive for his services such compensation as the board shall deem adequate, but not to exceed one thousand dollars per annum. The superintendent shall have the charge and control of the public schools of the city, subject to the orders, rules, regulations and by-laws of the board, and shall receive for his services such compensation as the board shall deem adequate.

Bond of Clerk.—SEC. 127. [Laws 1876, Ch. 122, Art. 10, Sec. 9.] Before entering upon the discharge of his duties, the clerk of the board of education shall give bond in the sum of one thousand dollars, with good and sufficient securities, to be approved by the board, and shall take and subscribe an oath or affirmation before a proper officer that he will support the constitution of the United States, the constitution of the state of Kansas, and faithfully perform the duties of his office.

Treasurer.—SEC. 128. [Laws 1876, Ch. 122, Art. 10, Sec. 10.] The treasurer of the city shall be, *ex officio*, the treasurer of the board of education; he shall attend all the meetings of the board when required so to do, shall prepare and submit, in writing, a monthly report of the state of its finances, and shall pay school moneys only upon a warrant signed by the président, or in his absence by the vice president, and countersigned by the clerk.

No Compensation.—SEC. 129. [Laws 1876, Ch. 122, Art. 10, Sec. 11.] No member of the board of education shall receive any pay or emolument for his services.

Examining Committee; Teachers.—SEC. 130. [Laws 1876, Ch. 122, Art. 10, Sec. 12.] The board of education, at such time as they shall deem expedient, shall appoint three competent persons, who shall be styled the examining committee of the board of education, whose duty it shall be to examine all persons who may apply to them as teachers; and no person shall be elected by the board as teacher who cannot produce a certificate from the examining committee, signed by all, or a majority of them, and setting forth that such person is competent to teach in such department of the public schools as may be stated in the certificate, and is a person of good moral character: *Provided*, That the board may elect as teacher a suitable person who holds a diploma or certificate from the state board of education.

Vacancy.—SEC. 131. [Laws 1876, Ch. 122, Art. 10, Sec. 13.] The board of education shall have power to fill any vacancy which may occur in the examining committee.

Annual Levy of School Tax.—SEC. 132. [Laws 1881, Ch. 149, Sec. 2.] The board of education shall, in the month of August in each year, prepare an estimate and levy of the amount of moneys necessary and requisite for the support and maintenance of the public schools under its charge, for the year commencing on the first day of January next thereafter, and also the amount necessary to pay the interest on bonds accruing during such year, and the amount of sinking fund necessary to be collected during such year for the payment and redemption of such bonds issued by said board, and shall cause to be certified by the president and clerk of the said board, to the county clerk of the county in which said city is situated, the percentage by them levied on the real and personal property of and within the said city as returned on the assessment roll of the county. And the said county clerk is hereby authorized and required to place the same on the tax roll of the county; and the said tax shall be collected by the county treasurer as the other taxes are collected, and when collected shall be paid to treasurer of the said city, for the sole purpose for which said taxes were levied, subject to the order of the said board of education; and all such levies required to be certified to the county clerk shall be so certified on or before the 25th day of August, annually: *Provided*, That the estimate and tax for the general purposes of the support and maintenance of such schools, and the expense thereof, shall not exceed in any one year seven mills on the dollar of all the taxable property of the said city: *Provided further*, The schools shall not be kept open more than nine months in any one year.

Taxes.—SEC. 133. [Laws 1876, Ch. 122, Art. 10, Sec. 15.] All taxes collected for the benifit of the public school shall be paid in money, and shall be placed in the hands of the city treasurer, subject to the order of the board of education.

District.—SEC. 134. [Laws 1876, Ch. 122, Art. 10, Sec. 16.] The whole city shall compose a school district for all purposes of taxation, but may be subdivided by the board of education into as many districts as they may think proper.

Property.—SEC. 135. [Laws 1876, Ch. 122, Art. 10, Sec. 17.] The title of all property held for the use or benefit of the public schools shall be vested in the board of education, and held by them in trust for the city; and the board of education may sue in its own name for all money due or to become due to the board or the school fund, and for any trespass upon, injury to, or concession of, any of the school property of said city for the benefit of the school fund of such city.

Sale of Property.—SEC. 136. [Laws 1876, Ch. 122, Art. 10, Sec. 18.] No school property of any kind shall be sold or conveyed by the board of education, except at a regular meeting of the same, and not then without an affirmative recorded vote of at least two-thirds of all the members of said board.

Meetings of the Board.—SEC. 137. [Laws 1876, Ch. 122, Art. 10, Sec. 19.] The regular meetings of the board of education shall be upon the first Monday in each month, but special meetings may be held from time to time, as circumstances may demand.

Annual Report.—SEC. 138. [Laws 1876, Ch. 122, Art. 10, Sec. 20.] The board of education, at the close of each school year, or as soon thereafter as practicable, shall make an annual report of the progress, prosperity and condition, financial as well as educational, of all the schools under their charge; and said report, or such portion of it as the board of education shall consider of advantage to the public, shall be printed either in a public newspaper or in pamphlet form.

Expenditures.—SEC. 139. [Laws 1876, Ch. 122, Art. 10, Sec. 21.] No expenditure, involving an amount greater than two hundred dollars, shall be voted, except in accordance with the provisions of a written contract.

Sectarian Doctrine.—SEC. 140. [Laws 1876, Ch. 122, Art. 10, Sec. 22.] No sectarian or religious doctrine shall be taught or inculcated in any of the public schools of the city; but nothing in this section shall be construed to prohibit the reading of the holy scriptures.

Exemptions.—SEC. 141. [Laws 1876, Ch. 122, Art. 10, Sec. 23.] All property held by the board of education for the use of public schools shall be exempt from taxation, and shall not be taken in any manner for any debt due from the city.

Bonds.—SEC. 142. [Laws 1876, Ch. 122, Art. 10, Sec. 24.] Whenever it shall be necessary to raise funds to purchase a school site or sites, or to erect or furnish suitable building or buildings thereon, or to provide for or pay any indebtedness already made or incurred for such purposes, it shall be lawful for the board of education to issue bonds and negotiate and sell the same, but at not less than ninety cents on the dollar. Such bonds shall bear date on the day they are issued and negotiated, and shall bear interest at a rate not exceeding ten per cent. per annum, payable semi-annually, and shall be payable in twenty years after their date: *Provided,* That no bond shall issue except by the vote of two-thirds of the members of such board at a regular meeting thereof: *And provided further,* That there shall not be outstanding at any one time more than one hundred and sixty thousand dollars in the aggregate amount of bonds issued by the board of education, under the authority hereby given, or otherwise.

Execution.—SEC. 143. [Laws 1876, Ch. 122, Art. 10, Sec. 25.] The bonds, the issuance of which is provided for in the preceding section, shall be signed by the president and clerk of the board of education, and countersigned by the treasurer; and said bonds shall specify the rate of interest, and the time when principal and interest shall be paid, and each bond so issued shall not be for a less sum than fifty dollars.

Levy for Interest and Sinking Fund.—SEC. 144. [Laws 1876, Ch. 122, Art. 10, Sec. 26.] The board of education, in its annual estimate as provided in this article, shall include an amount sufficient to pay the interest as the same accrues on all outstanding bonds issued by the board, and also to create a sinking fund for the redemption of said bonds, and shall levy and cause the same to be collected as provided in the first section of this act, in addition to the one-half of one per cent. authorized by the provisions of the said section for school purposes; and such moneys shall remain a specific fund for said purpose only, and shall not be appropriated for any other purpose, or in any other way, except as hereinafter provided.

Use of Sinking Fund.—SEC. 145. [Laws 1876, Ch. 122, Art. 10, Sec. 27.] The moneys levied and collected for creating a sinking fund for the redemption of the principal of the bonds issued by the board of education shall be used and employed or invested as follows:

First: After retaining an amount sufficient to pay the principal of any bonds maturing during the year, the board shall, with the surplus of such sinking fund, when the same shall be one thousand dollars or more, purchase any of the outstanding bonds issued by the board. Such purchase shall be made at the lowest price such bonds can be purchased at, but at not more than par value of such bonds, and whenever there shall be a surplus of such sinking fund amounting to the sum of one thousand dollars, the board shall purchase therewith like bonds, on the same terms and conditions hereinbefore specified.

Second: If for any reason such bonds cannot be purchased as hereinbefore specified, such sinking fund shall be invested by the treasurer, under the direction of the board of education, at such times as the board shall direct, in the interest-bearing bonds of the United States or the state of Kansas, which shall be purchased at the lowest market price. Interest accruing upon such bonds shall be invested in the same manner and for the same purpose as sinking fund. Such bonds shall be held by the treasurer until the principal of the bonds issued by the board of education shall become due, and shall then be sold at the highest market price and the proceeds applied to the payment of the bonds: *Provided,* That if at any time the board shall deem it best, it shall be lawful for such board to sell such bonds for the purpose of purchasing of the bonds issued by such board; but all such sales shall be at the highest market price, and the bonds of the board purchased with the proceeds of such sale shall be purchased at the lowest price they can be obtained for, and not above the par value of such bonds: *Provided,* That no bond issued by the board of education shall be purchased by said board that has not been outstanding five years: *And provided further,* That the bonds first maturing shall be first purchased, if they can be purchased on terms as favorable to the board as any others offered for sale to the said board. All bonds of the said board purchased under the authority hereby given, or paid by the board, shall be forthwith canceled and destroyed, and the clerk shall enter on the bond register of the said board, on the margin of the record of the said bonds, the date when the same were purchased and the price paid; and thereafter no interest or sinking fund shall be levied or collected for or on account of said bonds so canceled. Such sinking fund shall never be used nor appropriated in any other manner whatever.

Interest.—SEC. 146. [Laws 1876, Ch. 122, Art. 10, Sec. 28.] Whenever the interest of the above-mentioned bonds shall become due, the same shall be paid by the treasurer.

Security.—SEC. 147. [Laws 1876, Ch. 122, Art. 10, Sec. 29.] The credit of the school fund of such city is hereby pledged to the payment of the interest and principal of the bonds mentioned in this article, as the same may become due.

Bond Registry.—SEC. 148. [Laws 1876, Ch. 122, Art. 10, Sec. 30.] It shall be the duty of the clerk of the board of education to register, in a book provided for that purpose, the bonds issued under this act, which said registry shall show the number, date and amount, and to whom is made payable, each of said bonds.

Powers and Duties of Board of Education.—SEC. 149. [Laws 1879, Ch. 81, Sec. 1.] Section seventy-five of the act entitled "An act to incorporate cities of the first class," approved February twenty-fourth, eighteen hundred and sixty-eight, is hereby amended so that the same shall read and be as follows: Section 75. The board of education shall have power to elect their own officers, make all necessary rules for the government of the schools of said city under its charge and control, and of the said board, subject to the provisions of this act and the laws of this state; to organize and maintain separate schools for the education of white and colored children, except in the high school, where no discrimination shall be made on account of color; to exercise the sole control over the public schools and school property of said city; and shall have the power to establish a high school, and maintain the same in whole or in part, by demanding, collecting and receiving a tuition fee for and from each and every scholar or pupil attending such high school.

Organization of Board.—SEC. 150. [Laws 1879, Ch. 81, Sec. 2.] That section seventy-six of the act in the first section mentioned as amended by the act approved February tenth, eighteen hundred and sixty-nine, shall be amended so that the same shall read as follows: Section 76. The board of education shall, at its first regular meeting in August of each year, organize by the election of a president and vice president from its members, each of whom shall serve for one year, and until his successor is elected and qualified. They may elect a clerk, and a superintendent of public schools, neither of whom shall be a member of said board, and who shall hold their respective offices during the pleasure of the board. The board shall have the right, at any time and at any regular meeting, to hold an election to fill any vacancy which may occur among the officers of the board, or any of its agents, servants or employés. The fiscal year of such board shall close on the last day of June, and the annual reports of the president, superintendent, and of the several committees, shall be presented to the board on or before the first Monday in August in each year; and the term of office of the president and vice president of the year eighteen hundred and seventy-one, and of the several members of the board now in office, is extended so that their several terms of office shall expire on the first Monday of August, instead of the first Monday of May.

Refunding of Outstanding Bonded Debt.—Sec. 151. [Laws 1879, Ch. 81, Sec. 3.] The board of education of any city of the first class is hereby authorized and empowered to refund any and all outstanding bonds heretofore issued by or by order of the said board, by issuing new bonds to the holders of such outstanding bonds: *Provided*, That such new bonds shall not be for a greater amount than the par value of the bonds refunded. Such refunding bonds shall severally be in such amount as said board shall direct, and shall state for what purpose issued, and be payable to the person to whom issued, or bearer, within thirty years after date, in installments as hereinafter provided, and shall bear interest at the rate not exceeding six per cent. per annum, payable semi-annually on January first and July first. That there shall be attached to each of said bonds sixty coupons, numbered from one to sixty, and each of the first ten shall be for the amount of the semi-annual interest upon such bond. That said coupons numbered from eleven to thirty, both inclusive, shall be for the amount of six months' interest upon the principal of such bond unpaid, after deducting all installments of principal paid or provided for by prior maturing coupons, and one and seven-tenths per cent. of the principal sum mentioned in such bond; and the last thirty of such coupons shall each be for six months' interest upon the principal of said bond unpaid, after deducting all installments of principal paid or provided for by prior maturing coupons, and one-thirtieth of the principal of said bonds which shall remain unpaid at the end of fifteen years from the date of such bond or unprovided for by prior maturing coupons; and when the said coupons shall be fully paid the said bonds shall be of no further force or effect: *Provided*, That no bond or bonds hereby authorized shall be delivered until the bond or bonds to be surrendered therefor shall be surrendered and delivered to the said board. All bonds refunded under the provisions of this act shall be noted as surrendered and canceled on the registry of the said board, and the same shall be destroyed in the presence of said board.

Bonds Registered.—Sec. 152. [Laws 1879, Ch. 81, Sec. 4.] The bonds hereby authorized shall be numbered, and shall be registered in the book kept by said board for the registry of its bonds; and said bonds shall be signed by the president and clerk of said board, attested with the seal of said board by the clerk, and countersigned by the treasurer of said city.

Levy of Bond Tax.—Sec. 153. [Laws 1879, Ch. 81, Sec. 5.] The board of education, and any and all boards, body or officers, by law authorized to levy and collect taxes in and for said city for the support of schools therein, shall at the same time and in the same manner as the other taxes for school purposes are levied and collected, and in each and every year until said bonds and interest are fully paid, as hereinbefore provided, levy or cause to be levied upon all of the property within the said city subject to taxation for school purposes, a tax or taxes sufficient in amount to pay and discharge two of the coupons of each of the bonds issued under the provisions of this act, and then outstanding, and cause the same to be collected in the same manner as other school taxes are collected, and, with the moneys so collected, pay and discharge the coupons for which said tax or taxes were levied. And it shall be the duty of the clerk of said board to forthwith, on the payment of any such coupons, to note their payment upon the registry of said bonds, and present the same to the board, and in their presence cancel the same in such manner as the board shall direct; and said coupons shall be carefully preserved until the final payment of said bonds, and then destroyed, and the possession of such coupons by the board shall be conclusive evidence of their payment. And said board shall issue no bonds hereafter, except the refunding bonds provided for by this act.

Penalty.—Sec. 154. [Laws 1879, Ch. 81, Sec. 6.] If said board of education, or other board, body or officer, whose duty it shall be to levy taxes for the payment of ·the coupons of the said bonds, as herein provided, shall neglect or refuse to levy the tax or taxes for the payment of the coupons as by this act required, each member of such board or body, and each officer, who shall vote against or otherwise oppose the levy and collection of such tax or taxes, or shall do any act to prevent or delay such levy and collection, shall be liable, jointly and severally, to each and every holder of such bonds, or coupons of said bonds, which would have been payable from such taxes if the same had been levied for the whole amount unpaid on such coupons; and the same may be recovered in a civil action in any court of competent jurisdiction, and judgment rendered thereon may be collected and enforced in the same manner as other judgments are collected and enforced; and any such officer so neglecting or refusing to levy such tax shall also be deemed guilty of a misdemeanor, and on conviction thereof shall be fined in an amount equal to the amount which it may be shown should have been so levied during such year, or imprisoned in the county jail for a term not less than three nor more than twelve months.

Use of Money Levied and Collected under this Act.—Sec. 155. [Laws 1879, Ch. 81, Sec. 7.] Moneys levied and collected and received under and pursuant to this act shall not be used or employed for any other purpose than the payment of coupons of the bonds by this act

4

authorized; and any member of said board, or officer, who shall cause such money so collected to be used for any other purpose, temporary or otherwise, whatever, or counsel or consent to the same being so used, shall be liable, jointly and severally, to the holder of any of such bonds or coupons for any coupons due, to be recovered and collected as in section six hereof specified.

ARTICLE XI.—PUBLIC SCHOOLS IN CITIES OF THE SECOND CLASS.

Defined.—SEC. 156. [Laws 1876, Ch. 122, Art. 11, Sec. 1.] All cities now organized and acting as cities of the second class, by virtue of the authority of former acts, and all cities hereafter attaining a population over two thousand and not exceeding fifteen thousand inhabitants, shall be governed by the provisions of this act; and whenever any city shall have hereafter attained a population exceeding two thousand inhabitants, and such fact shall have been duly ascertained and certified by the proper authorities of such city to the governor, he shall declare, by public proclamation, such city subject to the provisions of this act. The mayor and council of such city shall, at the time of making the certificate herein provided for, make out and transmit to the governor an accurate description by metes and 'bounds of all the lands included within the limits of such city, and the additions thereto, if any.

Free Schools.—SEC. 157. [Laws 1876, Ch. 122, Art. 11, Sec. 2.] In each city governed by this act there shall be established and maintained a system of free common schools, which shall be kept open not less than three nor more than ten months in any one year, and shall be free to all children residing in such city between the ages of five and twenty-one years. But the board of education may, where school-room accommodations are insufficient, exclude for the time being, children between the ages of five and seven years.

Adjacent Territory.—SEC. 158. [Laws 1876, Ch. 122, Art. 11, Sec. 3.] Territory outside the city limits, but adjacent thereto, may be attached to such city for school purposes, upon application to the board of education of such city by a majority of the electors of such adjacent territory; and upon such application being made to the board of education, they shall, if they deem it proper and to the best ·interests of the schools of said city and the territory seeking to be attached, issue an order attaching such territory to such city for school purposes, and to enter the same upon their journal; and such territory shall, from the date of such order, be and compose a part of such city for school purposes only; and the taxable property of such adjacent territory shall be subject to taxation, and shall bear its full proportion of all expenses incurred in the erection of school buildings, and in maintaining the schools of such city. Whenever the territory so attached shall have attained a population equal to that of any one ward of such city, or whenever the taxable property of such attached territory shall equal that of any one ward of such city, such attached territory shall be entitled to elect two members of the board of education, who shall be elected at the same time that other members of the board are elected, by the qualified electors of such territory, at an election to be held at such place as the board of education may designate.

Body Corporate.—SEC. 159. [Laws 1876, Ch. 122, Art. 11, Sec. 4.] The public schools of each city organized in pursuance of this act shall be a body corporate, and shall possess the usual powers of a corporation for public purposes, by the name and style of "The board of education of the city of——, of the state of Kansas;" and in that name may sue or be sued, and be capable of contracting and being contracted with, of holding and conveying such real and personal estate as it may come into possession of, by will or otherwise, or as is authorized to be purchased by the provisions of this act.

Conveyance of Property —SEC. 160. [Laws 1876, Ch. 122, Art. 11, Sec. 5.] Any city of the second class is hereby authorized and required, upon the request of the board of education of such city, to convey to said board of education all property within the limits of any such city heretofore purchased by any such city for school purposes, and now held and used for such purposes, the title to which is vested in any such city.

How Executed.—SEC. 161. [Laws 1876, Ch. 122, Art. 11, Sec. 6.] All conveyances for the property mentioned in the preceding section shall be signed by the mayor and attested by the clerk of said city, and . shall have the seal of the city affixed thereto, and be acknowledged by the mayor of such city in the same manner as other conveyances of real estate.

Board of Education.—SEC. 162. [Laws 1876, Ch. 122, Art. 11, Sec. 6.] At each annual city election there shall be a board of education, consisting of two members from each ward, elected by the qualified voters thereof, one of whom shall be elected annually, and shall hold his office for the term of· two years, and until his successor is elected and qualified: *Provided,* That no member of the board of education shall be a member of the council, nor shall any member of the council be a member of the board of education.

Vacancy.—SEC. 163. [Laws 1876, Ch. 192, Art. 11, Sec. 8.] The board of education shall have power to fill any vacancy which may occur in their body: *Provided,* That any vacancy occurring more than ten days previous to the annual election, and having an unexpired term of one year, shall be filled at the first annual election thereafter ; and the ballots and returns of election shall be designated as follows: "To fill unexpired term."

Powers.—SEC. 164. [Laws 1876, Ch. 122, Art. 11, Sec. 9.] The board of education shall have power to elect their own officers, except the treasurer; to make their own rules and regulations, subject to the provisions of this article; to organize and maintain a system of graded schools; to establish a high school whenever in their opinion the educational interests of the city demand the same; and to exercise the sole control over the schools and school property of the city.

Organization.—SEC. 165. [Laws 1876, Ch. 122, Art. 11, Sec. 10.] The board of education, at its regular meeting in May of each year, shall organize by the election of a president and vice president from among its own members, each of whom shall serve for the term of one year, or until their successors are elected and qualified; they shall also elect a clerk, who shall hold his office during the pleasure of the board, and who shall receive such compensation for his services as the board may allow.

President.—SEC. 166. [Laws 1876, Ch. 122, Art. 11, Sec. 11.] It shall be the duty of the president to preside at all meetings of the board of education, to appoint all committees whose appointment is not otherwise provided for, and to sign all warrants ordered by the board of education to be drawn upon the treasurer for school moneys.

Vice President. —SEC. 167. [Laws 1876, Ch. 122, Art. 11, Sec. 12.] It shall be the duty of the vice president to perform all the duties of the president in case of his absence or disability.

Clerk. —SEC. 168. [Laws 1876, Ch. 122, Art. 11, Sec. 13.] It shall be the duty of the clerk to be present at all meetings of the board; to keep an accurate journal of its proceedings; to take charge of its books and documents; to countersign all warrants for school moneys drawn upon the treasurer by order of the board of education, and perform such other duties as the board of education or its committees may require.

Bond of Clerk.—SEC. 169. [Laws 1876, Ch. 122, Art. 11, Sec. 14.] Before entering upon the discharge of his duties, the clerk of the board of education shall give a bond in the sum of one thousand dollars, with good and sufficient sureties, to be approved by the board, conditioned for the faithful performance of the duties of his office.

Treasurer.—SEC. 170. [Laws 1876, Ch. 122, Art. 11, Sec. 15.] The treasurer shall prepare and submit in writing a monthly report of the state of the finances of the district; and shall, when required, produce at any meeting of the board, or any committee appointed for the purpose of examining his accounts, all books and papers pertaining to his office; he shall pay moneys only upon a warrant signed by the president, or in his absence by the vice president, and countersigned by the clerk; and shall execute a bond in such sum as the board may require, with sufficient sureties, to be approved by the board, conditioned for the faithful discharge of his duties of treasurer to such board.

Superintendent; Examining Committee; Teachers.—SEC. 171. [Laws 1876, Ch. 122, Art. 11, Sec. 16.] The board of education, at such times as they shall deem expedient, shall elect a superintendent of schools, in no case a member of their own body, whose duty it shall be to have a general supervision of the schools of the city, subject to the rules and regulations of the board, who shall hold his office during the pleasure of the board, and shall receive such compensation as that body may allow. The board shall also appoint two competent persons, who, with the superintendent as chairman thereof, shall be styled the examining committee of the board of education, whose duty it shall be to examine all persons who may apply to them as teachers; and no person except one who holds a diploma or a certificate from the state board of education, shall be elected by the board as teacher, who cannot produce a certificate from the examining committee signed by all or a majoriy of them, and setting forth that such person is competent to teach in such department of the public schools as may be stated in the certificate, and is a person of good moral character; and the board may fill any vacancy which may occur in the examining committee.

Annual School Tax.—SEC. 172. [Laws 1876, Ch. 122, Art. 11, Sec. 18.] The board of education shall, on or before the fifteenth day of August of each year, levy a tax for the support of the schools of the city for the fiscal year next ensuing, not exceeding in any one year eight mills on the dollar on all personal, mixed and real property within the district which is taxable according to the laws of the state of Kansas, which levy shall be approved by the city council; and which levy, when so approved, the clerk of the board shall certify to the county clerk, who is hereby authorized and required to place the same on the tax roll of said county, to be collected by the treasurer of the county as are other taxes, and paid over by him to the treasurer of the board of education, of whom he shall take receipt in duplicate, one of which he shall file in his office, and the other he shall forthwith transmit to the clerk of the board of education.

Taxable Property.—SEC. 173. [Laws 1876, Ch. 122, Art. 11, Sec. 19.] The taxable property of the whole city, including the territory attached for school purposes, shall be subject to taxation. All taxes collected for the benefit of the schools shall be paid in money, and shall be placed in the hands of the treasurer, subject to the order of the board of education.

Meetings of the Board.—SEC. 174. [Laws 1876, Ch. 122, Art. 11, Sec. 20.] The regular meetings of the board of education shall be upon the first Monday of each month, but special meetings may be held from time to time, as circumstances may demand.

Annual Report.—SEC. 175. [Laws 1876, Ch. 122, Art. 11, Sec. 21.] The board of education, at the close of each school year, or as soon thereafter as practicable, shall make an annual report of the progress, prosperity and condition, financial as well as educational, of all the schools under their charge; and said report, or such portion of it as the board of education shall consider of advantage to the public, shall be printed, either in a public newspaper or in pamphlet form.

Expenditures; Contracts.—SEC. 176. [Laws 1876, Ch. 122, Art. 11, Sec. 22.] No expenditures involving an amount greater than two hundred dollars shall be made except in accordance with the provisions of a written contract, and no contract involving an expenditure of more than five hundred dollars for the purpose of erecting any public buildings or making any improvements shall be made except upon sealed proposals, and to the lowest responsible bidder.

Sectarian Doctrine.—SEC. 177. [Laws 1876, Ch. 122, Art. 11, Sec. 23.] No sectarian doctrine shall be taught or inculcated in any of the public schools of the city; but the holy scriptures, without note or comment, may be used therein.

Bond.—SEC. 178. [Laws 1876, Ch. 122, Art. 11, Sec. 24.] Whenever it shall become necessary, by the board of education, in order to raise sufficient funds for the purchase of a school site or sites, or to erect a suitable building or buildings thereon, or to fund any bonded indebtedness, it shall be lawful for the board of education of every city coming under the provisions of this act to borrow money, for which they are hereby authorized and empowered to issue bonds bearing a rate of interest not exceeding ten per cent. per annum, payable annually or semi-annually, at such place as may be mentioned upon the face of said bonds, which bonds shall be payable in not more than twenty years from their date; and the board of education is hereby authorized and empowered to sell such bonds at not less than ninety cents on the dollar: *Provided*, That no bonds shall be issued until the question shall be submitted to the people, and a majority of the qualified electors who shall vote on the question at an election called for that purpose shall have declared by their votes in favor of issuing such bonds.

Bond Election.—SEC. 179. [Laws 1876, Ch. 122, Art. 11, Sec. 25.] It shall be the duty of the mayor of each city governed by this act, upon the request of the board of education, forthwith to call an election, to be conducted in all respects as are the elections for city officers in the same cities, except that the returns shall be made to the board of education for the purpose of taking the sense of such district upon the question of issuing such bonds, naming in the proclamation of such election the amount of bonds asked for, and the purpose for which they are to be issued.

Execution of Bonds.—SEC. 180. [Laws 1876, Ch. 122, Art. 11, SEC. 26.] The bonds, the issuance of which is provided for in the foregoing section, shall be signed by the president, attested by the clerk and countersigned by the treasurer of the board of education; and said bonds shall specify the rate of interest and the time when principal and interest shall be paid, and each bond so issued shall be for a sum not less than fifty dollars.

Levy for Interest and Sinking Funds.—SEC. 181. [Laws 1876, Ch. 122, Art. 11, Sec. 27.] The board of education, at the time of its annual levy of taxes for the support of schools, as hereinbefore provided, shall also levy a sufficient amount to pay the interest as the same accrues on all bonds issued under the provisions of this article, and also to create a sinking fund for the redemption of said bonds, which it shall levy and collect, in addition to the rate per cent. authorized by the provisions aforesaid for school purposes; and said amount of funds, when paid into the treasury, shall be and remain a specific fund for said purpose only, and shall not be appropriated in any other way except as hereinafter provided.

Use of Sinking Fund.—SEC. 182. [Laws 1876, Ch. 122, Art. 11, Sec. 28.] All moneys raised for the purpose of creating a sinking fund for the final redemption of all bonds issued under this article, shall be invested annually by the board of education in bonds of the state of Kansas, or of the United States, or the board may buy and cancel the bonds of the district whenever such may be purchased at or below par.

Interest.—SEC. 183. [Laws 1876, Ch. 122, Art. 11, Sec. 29.] Whenever the interest coupons of the bonds hereinbefore authorized shall become due, they shall be promptly paid on presentation, by the treasurer, out of money in his hands collected for that purpose; and he shall indorse upon the face of such coupons in red ink the word " Paid," and the date of payment, and sign the initials of his name.

Security.—SEC. 184. [Laws 1876, Ch. 122, Art. 11, Sec. 30.] The school fund and property of such city and territory attached for school purposes is hereby pledged to the payment of the interest and principal of the bonds mentioned in this article, as the same may become due.

Bond Registry.—SEC. 185. [Laws 1876, Ch. 122, Art. 11, Sec. 31.] It shall be the duty of the clerk of the board of education to register in a book provided for that purpose the bonds issued under this article, and all warrants issued by the board, which said register shall show the number, date and amount of said bonds, and to whom made payable.

Oath of Office.—SEC. 186. [Laws 1876, Ch. 122, Art. 11, Sec. 32.] Each member of the board of education and officer provided for in this article shall take and subscribe an oath or affirmation to support the constitution of the United States, the constitution of the State of Kansas, and faithfully to perform the duties of his office. The oath and bond of the clerk shall be filed with the treasurer; all other oaths and bonds shall be filed with the clerk.

Treasurer of the Board.—SEC. 187. [Laws 1879, Ch. 83, Sec. 1.] There shall be elected on the first Tuesday of April, eighteen hundred and seventy-nine, and every year thereafter, such councilmen, members of the board of education, justices of the peace and constables, as are required by law to be chosen at such election; and at such first election as herein provided, and on every alternate year thereafter, there shall be elected a mayor, city treasurer, police judge, city attorney, *and treasurer of the board of education.* The mayor shall appoint, by and with the consent of the council, a city marshal, a city clerk and city assessor, and may appoint an assistant marshal, city engineer, street commissioner, and such policemen and other officers as they may deem necessary. The officers so appointed and confirmed shall hold their offices for the term of one year, aud until their successors are appointed and qualified. The council shall by ordinance specify their duties and compensation, and by ordinance abolish any office created by them whenever they may deem it expedient. The councilmen, members of the board of education, justices of the peace, mayor, city treasurer, police judge, city attorney, and treasurer of the board of education, shall hold their offices for the term of two years, and all other officers for the term of one year: *Provided,* At the first annual election after the organization of any city there shall be two councilmen and two members of the board of education .elected from each ward, one of whom shall serve for one year and one for two years, and one councilman and one member of the board of education shall be elected from each ward at each annual election thereafter: *Provided,* That no member of the board of education shall be a member of the council, nor shall any member of the council be a member of the board of education.

ARTICLE XII.—Public Schools in Cities of the Third Class.

§188. Cities of the third class defined; government §189. Shall not be detached for school districts, etc
of public schools.

Defined.—Sec. 188. [Laws 1876, Ch. 122, Art. 12, Sec. 1.] Public schools in incorporated cities which have not less than two hundred and fifty and not over two thousand inhabitants, 'if not otherwise provided for by law, shall be governed by the provisions of this act which apply to the organization and maintenance of district schools or of union or graded schools.

Area.—Sec. 189. [Laws 1876, Ch. 122, Art. 12, Sec. 2.] That no portion of the corporation of a city of the third class shall be detached from the school district in which the city is located, and the whole of such corporation shall be and remain in one school district for the purpose of schools and taxation.

ARTICLE XIII.—School-District Bonds.

§190. Purposes for which district bonds may be issued, and restrictions concerning the same.
191. Bond elections; notices of, and how conducted.
192. Denominations, rates of interest, and disposal of bonds.
193. Bonds must be registered.
194. Sinking fund, how provided and invested.
195. Penalty for issuing bonds without authority, and for misappropriation of the proceeds.
196. Final disposition of paid bonds and coupons.
197. Districts not affected by this act.
198. Bond laws repealed.
199. The time of payment of bonds belonging to the state permanent school fund may be extended.

§200. Bonds belonging to the state permanent school fund may be paid before maturity.
201. Payment of bonds belonging to the state permanent school fund to be made to the state treasurer.
202. State treasurer to inform county and city treasurers of bonds belonging to the state permanent school fund.
203. Remittance of funds to state treasurer.
204. Bonds to be canceled by state treasurer.
205. Penalty for city and county treasurers refusing to act.

School-District Bonds.—SEC. 190. [Laws 1879, Ch. 49, Sec. 1.]

That for the purpose of erecting or purchasing one or more school houses in and for any school district in the state of Kansas, the board of directors of the same shall have power to issue the bonds of the district in an amount not to exceed five per cent. of its taxable property, as shown in the last assessment thereof. And for the purpose of extending the time of payment of the bonded indebtedness of any school district, the board of directors of the same shall have the power to issue the bonds of the district in a sum not to exceed in amount its outstanding bonded indebtedness: *Provided,* That no such bonds shall be issued until, at an election called for that purpose, the question shall have been submitted to the qualified electors of the district, and a majority of all the qualified electors in the district shall have declared by their votes in favor of issuing the same: *And provided further,* That no such election shall be ordered unless a petition stating the purpose for which the bonds are to be issued and signed by at least one-third of the qualified electors of said district, and in no case less than ten qualified electors of said district, shall have been presented to the district board, praying that a vote be taken for the issuing of such amount of bonds as may be asked for therein: *And provided further,* That it shall be unlawful for any school district to create any bonded indebtedness unless there are at least twenty-five persons between the ages of five and twenty-one years actually residing within the limits thereof, as shown by a sworn census return, taken by the direction of the board of directors of such school district.

Election.—SEC. 191. [Laws 1879, Ch. 49, Sec. 2.] Whenever such a petition, so signed, shall be presented to the board of directors of any school district, praying that a vote be taken on the question of issuing the bonds of the said district, it shall be the duty of the district board immediately to order an election for the purpose of determining the question of the issuing of the bonds as prayed for, and forthwith to give notice by posting up written or printed notices signed by the clerk, in five of the most public places in the district, which notices shall be posted up at least ten days before such election, and shall state therein the object for which the election was called and the manner in which the question shall be voted upon. The said election shall be conducted in all respects as are general elections under the laws of the state, except that females of the age of twenty-one years shall be entitled to vote at all such elections, subject only to the exceptions applied to males; and the returns of the election shall be the same, except that they shall be made to the district board.

Issuance.—SEC. 192. [Laws 1879, Ch. 49, Sec. 3.] The bonds herein provided for shall be issued in denominations of not less than one hundred dollars nor more than five hundred dollars each; they shall bear interest at a rate not to exceed seven per cent. per annum, payable semi-annually, on the first days of January and July of each year, at such place as shall be designated in the bonds, the principal of the bonds being made payable within fifteen years from their date. These bonds shall specify on their face the date of issue, amount, for what purpose and to whom issued, the time they run, the rates and times of payment of interest, and shall have coupons attached for the interest as it becomes due, said coupons being so arranged that the last one shall fall due at the time of the maturity of the bond. Said bonds and the coupons thereto attached shall be signed by the director and countersigned by the clerk, and after registration by the county clerk, shall be negotiable and transferable by delivery, and may be disposed of by the district board at not less than ninety-five cents on the dollar, and the proceeds of the same applied as provided for in the petition at which issuance of the bonds was authorized.

Registration.—SEC. 193. [Laws 1879, Ch. 49, Sec. 4.] Before delivering any school-district bonds, the board of directors of the district issuing the same shall cause them to be registered with the clerk of the county in which the said district is located. And it shall be the duty of the county clerk, on presentation of any school bonds for registry, to register the same in a book prepared for that purpose, which register shall contain, first, the number of the district; second, the number of the bond; third, date of bond; fourth, to whom payable; fifth, when [where] payable; sixth, when due; seventh, when interest is due; eighth, amount of bond. The county clerk shall furnish one copy of his register to the county treasurer, and forward one copy to the state superintendent, together with a statement, showing, first, the number of sections of land in the district issuing such bonds; second, the number of acres of land assessed and subject to taxation in said district; third, the assessed valuation of taxable lands; fourth, the assessed valuation of all personal property in such district; which statement shall be signed by each member of the school board issuing the bonds, and the county clerk shall certify under the official seal of his office to the correctness of the statement and the genuineness of the signatures attached thereto.

Interest and Sinking Fund.—SEC. 194. [Laws 1879, Ch. 49, Sec. 5.] It shall be the duty of the board of county commissioners of each county to levy, annually, upon all the taxable property in each district in such county a tax sufficient to pay the interest accruing upon any bond issued by such district, and to provide a sinking fund for the final redemption of the bonds, such levy to be made with the annual levy of the county, and the taxes collected with other taxes, and when collected shall be and remain in the hands of the county treasurer, a specific fund for the payment of the interest upon such bonds, and for their final payment at maturity: *Provided,* That moneys in the hands of the county treasurer belonging to the sinking funds of the several school districts in such county shall be invested by the county treasurer, first, in the bonds of the district to which said sinking fund belongs, provided such bonds can be purchased at a price not exceeding their market or par value; second, in the bonds of other school districts of this state maturing before the bonds for which such fund is raised, provided the same can be purchased at a price not exceeding their market or par value; third, in the bonds of the state of Kansas, or of the United States.

Penalty.—SEC. 195. [Laws 1879, Ch. 49, Sec. 6.] If any school-district officer, whose duty it is under the provisions of this act to issue or assist in any manner in the issuance of the bonds of any school district, shall prepare, sign or deliver, or aid, counsel or assist in preparing, signing or delivering, or shall cause to be prepared, signed or delivered, any bond or bonds of any school district, at any time before such bond or bonds are authorized by this act to be prepared, signed or delivered, such officer shall be guilty of a felony, and upon conviction shall be fined in a sum of not less than five hundred dollars nor more than five thousand dollars, or by imprisonment in the penitentiary for not less than one year and not longer than five years, or by both such fine and imprisonment. And if the board of directors of any school district, or any member thereof, shall use or dispose of any school-district bonds, or the money accruing from the sale of such bonds, in any other manner or for any other purpose than that for which the same was created or intended, he or they shall be liable to be punished by fine in any sum not less than one thousand dollars, by information or indictment in any court of competent jurisdiction, or by imprisonment in the county jail not more than six months, or by both such fine and imprisonment.

Final Disposition.—SEC. 196. [Laws 1879, Ch. 49, Sec. 7.] On the payment of the bonds or coupons of any school district, the county treasurer shall immediately cancel the same, and indorse thereon the date of payment; and at the time of his settlements with the several school-district treasurers of his county, he shall deliver to each the canceled bonds and coupons of his district, and take a receipt therefor, and such canceled bonds and coupons shall be destroyed by the district treasurer in the presence of all the officers of the district, a complete record of their destruction being made by the district clerk. On the last Sat-

urday of July of each year, each and every county treasurer shall make
to the clerk of his county a detailed report of all the bonds and coupons
canceled during the year, and the date of payment of the same, accompanied by the receipts given by district treasurers therefor; and the
county clerk shall immediately thereafter cancel the registry of all such
bonds and coupons by indorsing thereon the date of payment of each.

Rights Saved.—SEC. 197. [Laws 1879, Ch. 49, Sec. 8.] The provisions of this act shall not apply to any school district where any election has already been held for the purpose of authorizing the issue of
school-district bonds, but the same shall be issued as now provided by
law.

Repealing Clause.—SEC. 198. [Laws 1879, Ch. 49, Sec. 9.] Article thirteen of chapter one hundred and twenty-two, laws of eighteen
hundred and seventy-six; section five of chapter one hundred and twenty-
four, laws of eighteen hundred and seventy-four; chapter one hundred
and twenty-four, laws of eighteen hundred and seventy-six; and chapter
forty-four, laws of eighteen hundred and seventy-seven, are hereby
repealed.

Time Extended.—SEC. 199. [Laws 1879, Ch. 160, Sec. 1.] The
board of commissioners for the management of the state permanent school
funds shall have the power, and it is hereby made the duty of said board,
to exchange any school-district bonds belonging to the permanent school
funds now in the state treasury, for other bonds of the same district bearing a lower rate of interest, and running a longer time than the bonds
exchanged: *Provided,* That they shall not purchase any funding bonds
running a less time than five years: *And provided further,* That the rate
of interest on bonds running from five to fifteen years shall be seven per
cent. per annum; and on bonds running longer than fifteen years the rate
of interest shall be six per cent. per annum.

Payment before Maturity.—SEC. 200. [Laws 1879, Ch. 160,
Sec. 2.] If at any time any board of education or school district shall have
accumulated in the treasury sinking fund sufficient to pay in full any
bond or bonds issued by such board or district before their maturity, the
permanent school fund being the holders thereof, such board of education or school district may pay the same to the state treasurer and take
up such bond or bonds, and the state treasurer is hereby authorized to
receive the same, and to cancel such bond or bonds and the unmatured
coupons attached thereto, and deliver the same, so canceled, to the officer paying the amount: *Provided,* That the state treasurer, before delivering said bond or bonds, shall present the same to the auditor of state,
together with a statement showing the amount of coupons upon which
no moneys have been received; and upon examining such statement,

and comparing it with the coupons attached to such bond or bonds, the auditor shall credit the treasury with the amounts shown to be canceled before maturity: *Provided,* That nothing in this section shall be construed to apply to bonds exchanged under the provision of section one of this act.

Payable at State Treasury.—SEC. 201. [Laws 1877, Ch. 174, Sec. 1.] From and after the passage of this act, the interest and principal of all bonds now belonging or which may hereafter belong to the permanent school fund or sinking fund of the state of Kansas, which have been or may hereafter be issued under and pursuant to the laws of said state, shall be payable at the office of the state treasurer.

State Treasurer.—SEC. 202. [Laws 1877, Ch. 174, Sec. 2.] At least thirty days before the maturity of any bonds or coupons belonging to the permanent school fund or sinking fund, it shall be the duty of the state treasurer to furnish a detailed statement to each county or city treasurer, or the treasurer of any board of education, of the amount due from them respectively, describing in such statement the number of the district or the name of the city, the amount of interest due, and the amount of principal due, if any.

County and City Treasurers.—SEC. 203. [Laws 1877, Ch. 174, Sec. 3.] It shall be the duty of each county and city treasurer, and the treasurers of boards of education, to remit to the state treasurer, at least ten days before the maturity of any bonds or coupons, all moneys collected by them for the redemption of such bonds and coupons ; and all express charges and postage shall be a proper charge against such city or school district, and shall be allowed to such treasurer on settlement.

Cancellation.—SEC. 204. [Laws 1877, Ch. 174, Sec. 4.] On receipt of any funds by the state treasurer, he shall immediately cancel all coupons or bonds for which funds are remitted, and return such coupons or bonds to the office of the treasurer remitting for the same.

Penalty.—SEC. 205. [Laws 1877, Ch. 174, Sec. 5.] Any county or city treasurer, or treasurer of any board of education, who shall neglect or refuse to perform the duties required of him by this act, shall be liable to the state in a sum equal to double the amount of such bonds or coupons remaining unpaid by reason of such neglect or refusal, which may be recovered in a suit at law against such treasurer and his bondsmen ; and it is hereby made the duty of the county attorney of the proper county, upon the request of the attorney general, to prosecute all such suits.

May be Sold.—SEC. 206. [Laws 1876, Ch. 122, Art. 14, Sec. 1.] All lands granted by the congress of the United States for school purposes, known as sections sixty [sixteen] and thirty-six, together with all such as have been granted in lieu of said sections, may be sold, and such sale shall be regulated by the provisions of this act.

Appraisement.—SEC. 207. [Laws 1876, Ch. 122, Art. 14, Sec. 2.] Whenever twenty householders of any organized township in which the land is situated, shall petition the superintendent of public schools of such county to expose to sale any portion or portions of said land, describing the same, he shall, by and with the consent of the county commissioners of his county, appoint, in writing, three disinterested householders, residing in the county in which said land is situated, who, being first duly sworn by an officer authorized to administer oaths, to faithfully perform their duties, shall appraise each legal subdivision of

said land separately at its real value, and return their appraisement in
writing, signed by them, to the clerk of the county; and in case any
parcel of the said lands shall have been improved, the said appraisers
shall, in addition to the appraisement of the land, return and file with
the same a separate appraisement of the improvements upon the land:
Provided, That no appraisement of land for less than three dollars per
acre shall be of any validity or entitle any person to the provisions of
this act.

County Clerk.—SEC. 208. [Laws 1876, Ch. 122, Art. 14, Sec. 3.]
The county clerk shall immediately file the said appointment and appraisement of said appraisers in his office, and record the same in a book
kept for that purpose.

Settlers' Rights.—SEC. 209. [Laws 1876, Ch. 122, Art. 14, Sec. 4.]
Any person who has settled upon and improved any portion of school
lands prior to the appraisement, may, within sixty days from its appraisement, file in the probate court of his county a petition, stating that
he has settled upon and improved said lands; that the same have been
appraised, and the amount of the appraisement, and asking that he be
allowed to purchase the same: *Provided*, That the heirs of deceased
persons who have made improvements upon said lands shall be entitled
to all the rights accruing to actual residents thereon.

Proceedings in Probate Court.—SEC. 210. [Laws 1876, Ch. 122,
Art. 14, Sec. 5.] Said court shall require the petitioner to prove the
facts set forth in his petition, and the superintendent of public instruction may appear and introduce testimony to controvert said facts; and if
said petitioner fails to establish the truth of his petition, he shall be adjudged to pay the costs. If he feels himself aggrieved by the decision
of said court, he shall have the right to appeal to the district court, by
filing a bond within fifteen days after such decision, conditioned that he
will prosecute the appeal, and pay all damages and costs that may be adjudged against him. The state shall have power to appeal from the
decision of said court, by the superintendent filing a notice thereof,
within the time prescribed for the appeal by the petitioner; and when
said notice shall have been filed, the appeal shall be granted, and the
probate court shall transmit to the clerk of the district court a certified
transcript of the record and proceedings relating to the cause, together
with the original papers in his office relating thereto; and the district

SEC. 209. Improvements upon school land entitle the owner to no special privileges as a purchaser,
unless accompanied by actual settlement, made prior to the appraisement.

A person who has settled upon and improved any portion of school lands prior to the appraisement,
cannot, before he has actually become the purchaser of the same, lawfully remove mineral or timber
from the same, even for use upon or improvement of said lands. See section 219, and section 231-237
of this article.

court shall have jurisdiction of the cause, and shall proceed to hear, try, and determine the same anew, without regard to any error, defect, or other imperfection in the proceedings in the probate court.

Notice of Sale, etc.—SEC. 211. [Laws 1876, Ch. 122, Art. 14, Sec. 6.] In all cases where the court shall find that the petitioner has settled upon and improved school lands, as set forth in his petition, the petitioner may purchase the said lands, not exceeding one quarter-section, for the appraised value thereof, exclusive of the value of the improvements. The county treasurer shall then offer the unsold portion of all school lands for sale at public auction, after giving four weeks' notice thereof in some newspaper published in such county; and in case no such paper is published in such county, then said notice shall be given by posting the same at each voting precinct in such county at least four weeks previous to the sale; (and that any person may and shall have the privilege of making a bid or offer for said lands, between the hours of ten o'clock A. M. and three o'clock P. M. of said day of sale.) Said notice shall contain a description of the land and improvements, if any, thereon, with the appraised value thereof, and a statement (of the hours of sale, which shall be between the hours of ten o'clock A. M. and three o'clock P. M., as aforesaid,) and the place of sale; and no bid at said sale shall be received for less than the appraised value of said land and improvements. Timber land may be subdivided into lots of such size as the superintendent of public instruction and appraisers may deem best; and in all cases one-half the purchase-money for timber land shall be paid at the time of purchase, and the purchaser shall give a good and sufficient bond for the payment of the remainder, as for other lands sold under this act.

Terms of Payment.—SEC. 212. [Laws 1879, Ch. 162, Sec. 1.] Any person purchasing such land shall pay to the treasurer of the county in which the same is situate, one-tenth of the amount of the purchase-money, taking therefor a receipt, which he shall present to the county clerk, together with a bond in double the amount of the purchase-money unpaid, conditioned that he will not commit waste upon said land, and that he will pay the balance of said purchase-money in twenty years, and interest to be paid annually thereon at the rate of seven per cent. per annum, as the same becomes due: *Provided,* That the purchaser may pay the balance of the purchase-money at any time, or in installments of not less than twenty-five dollars: *Provided, also,* Any person having heretofore purchased such land and made partial payment of the purchase-money thereof, and who has not defaulted in the payment of interest and taxes due upon such purchase, may, upon the expiration of the time when the unpaid part of such purchase-money becomes due, have the

5

time of said final payment extended twenty years, by presenting to the county clerk of the county in which said land is situate a new bond in double the amount of the purchase-money remaining unpaid, said bond conditioned the same as the bond aforementioned in this section.

Certificate of Purchase.—SEC. 213. [Laws 1876, Ch. 122, Art. 14, Sec. 8.] The county clerk shall thereupon enter the amount of the purchase-money on the land, the amount paid upon the same, in a book kept for that purpose, and shall charge the same to the county treasurer in the records of the county, and shall issue to the purchaser a certificate, under the seal of his office, showing the amount paid, the amount due, and the time when due, with interest, and that upon the payment of said amount, when due, with interest, he will be entitled to a patent to said land. It shall be the duty of the attorney general to prepare a proper form for said certificates for the sale of said land, so as to protect the rights of the state and of the purchaser, his heirs and assigns.

Interest, How Applied.—SEC. 214. [Laws 1876, Ch. 122, Art. 14, Sec. 9.] The interest on the deferred payments of the lands sold under this act shall be annually appropriated to the support of schools, as other school moneys, under the direction of the state superintendent of public instruction, as provided by law.

Credits.—SEC. 215. [Laws 1876, Ch. 122, Art. 14, Sec. 10.] The purchaser, when he pays to the county treasurer the interest, as it becomes due, or any portion of the principal, shall take a receipt for the same, which he shall present to the county clerk, who shall credit him with the same, and charge the amount to the treasurer.

Abstracts.—SEC. 216. [Laws 1876, Ch. 122, Art. 14, Sec. 11.] The county clerk shall, semi-annually, on the first days of January and July of each year, transmit to the state auditor an abstract of the land for which he has issued certificates during the year, the amount of the purchase-money for the same, the amount paid on each parcel of land, and the amount paid on yearly installments for the current year, principal and interest separately.

State Auditor.—SEC. 217. [Laws 1876, Ch. 122, Art. 14, Sec. 12.] The auditor shall charge each of the treasurers in the state the amount of moneys received as principal and interest, separately, from the sale of school lands in their respective counties, as certified by the clerks of the several counties, and upon the payment of the said moneys to the treasurer of state, and the presentation of the state treasurer's receipt, shall credit the several treasurers with the amount of the same.

County Treasurers.—SEC. 218. [Laws 1876, Ch. 122, Art. 14, Sec. 13.] The treasurers of the several counties shall pay over, semi-annually, to the treasurer of the state, the amount received in their counties from the sale of school land, taking receipts therefor, which, when indorsed by the auditor of state, shall be presented to the clerk of his county, who shall credit him with the amount of the same; and any treasurer failing so to do shall be liable in double the amount not paid over, on his official bond, to be recovered by action in the district court, in the name of the state of Kansas.

Waste; Taxation.—SEC. 219. [Laws 1879, Ch. 161, Sec. 1.] No purchaser of school land, prior to his obtaining title to the same, shall commit any waste upon such land, or take or remove mineral or timber from the same, other than for use upon or improvements of said land. The lands purchased under this act shall be subject to taxation, as other lands; and in case of non-payment of any taxes charged thereon, the said lands may be sold, as in other cases, but the purchaser at such sale shall be subject to all the conditions of the bond of the original maker, and of the certificate of purchase: *Provided*, That such purchaser of said school land shall be allowed one year from the date of the certificate of sale of such land for such taxes, in which to redeem from such tax sale, by complying with the provisions of law relating to the redemption of land from tax sale, and paying to the county treasurer, for the benefit of the holder of such tax certificate, all installments of interest or other payments which such holder of tax certificate has been compelled to pay in order to prevent a forfeiture of the rights of purchaser of school land, under the provisions of section sixteen of this act.

Patent.—SEC. 220. [Laws 1876, Ch. 122, Art. 14, Sec. 15.] On presentation of a certificate of the county clerk, showing that any person has paid the full amount of the purchase-money, and all interest due, for any portion of said school lands, with a certificate thereon, indorsed by the auditor of state, showing that he has charged the county treasurer of the county where the land is situated with the full amount of the purchase-money mentioned in said certificate, the governor of the state shall issue a patent to the purchaser, his heirs or assigns, for the same, which said patent shall convey to the patentee a full title in fee simple to said lands.

Forfeiture; Fees.—SEC. 221. [Laws 1879, Ch. 161, Sec. 2.] If any purchaser of school land shall fail to pay the annual interest when the same becomes due, or the balance of the purchase-money when the same becomes due, it shall be the duty of the county clerk of the county in which such land is situated, immediately to issue to the purchaser a notice in writing, notifying such purchaser of such default, and that if such purchaser fail to pay, or cause to be paid, the amount so due, together with the costs of issuing and serving such notice, within sixty days from the service thereof, the said purchaser, and all persons claiming under him, will forfeit absolutely all right and interest in and to such land under said purchase, and an action will be brought to eject such purchaser, and all persons claiming under him, from such land. It shall be the duty of said county clerk to include in such notice all tracts of land sold to the same purchaser, and on which default in any such payment then exists. The notice above provided for shall be served by the sheriff of the county, by delivering a copy thereof to such purchaser, if found in the county—also to all persons in possession of such land; and if such purchaser cannot be found, and no person is in possession of said land, then by posting the same up in a conspicuous place in the office of the county clerk. And in case such land or any part thereof has been sold for taxes, a copy of such notice shall be delivered to such purchaser at tax sale, if a resident of the county. Said sheriff shall serve such notice and make due return of the time and manner of such service within fifteen days from the time of his receipt of the same. The sheriff shall be entitled to the same fees and mileage for serving the same as allowed by law for serving summons in civil actions. If such purchaser shall fail to pay the sum so due, and all costs incident to the issue and service of said notice, within sixty days from the time of the service or posting of such notice as above provided, such purchaser and all persons claiming under him shall forfeit absolutely all rights and interest in and to such land, under and by virtue of such purchase. And the county attorney shall proceed to eject him and all persons claiming under him from said premises, if in possession. If the costs of the issue and service of the notice above provided for be not paid by the purchaser of such land, the same shall be paid by the county treasurer out of the proceeds of the sale of school lands in his hands, upon the order of the county superintendent of public instruction, made upon the affidavits of the officers to whom the same are due, showing the amount and correctness of the same: *Provided,* In all cases of the sale of school lands heretofore made, when the purchaser or purchasers thereof have made partial payments therefor, and have forfeited the same by law, and the money already paid thereon, and when the said purchaser or purchasers thereof have not been ejected, the person or persons having made such partial payment or payments, their heirs or assigns, may renew their right to retain said lands by making full payment of all interest that may be due, with interest at the rate of ten per cent. per annum on all interest in default from the date of default to date of full payment: *Provided,* Such payment shall be made within six months from the first day of April, 1879: *And provided,* When such lands shall have been disposed of to other persons, in pursuance of law, no interest obtained shall be affected by this act: *And provided further,* That all expenses that may be incurred under this act shall be borne by those seeking to avail themselves of the benefits of this act.

Forfeited Lands.—SEC. 222. [Laws 1879, Ch. 161, Sec. 3.] Land from which purchasers have been ejected, and lands which have been forfeited, and which are unoccupied by the purchaser or his assigns, shall be reappraised, and may be purchased by any person in accordance with the provisions of this act, and in all cases lands which have not been claimed or purchased shall be reappraised every five years : *Provided,* That they may be reappraised at any time on petition of one-half of the *bona fide* householders of the township in which the lands lie to the board of county commissioners of the county, at their discretion. But such reappraisement shall be conducted according to the provisions of this act, and the sales upon the same shall be conducted in all respects in accordance with the provisions of this act.

Unlawful Purchase.—SEC. 223. [Laws 1876, Ch. 122, Art. 14, Sec. 18.] It shall be unlawful for the county superintendent appointing the appraisers, or the persons appraising the lands, to purchase, either directly or indirectly, any portion of the lands appraised by them.

Investment of Proceeds.—SEC. 224. [Laws 1876, Ch. 122, Art. 14, Sec. 19.] The proceeds of the sale of school lands shall be invested by the board of commissioners for the management and investment of school funds, in the bonds or other interest-paying securities of this state or of the United States, at the current market price thereof, at the time of making such investment.

Private Sale.—SEC. 225. [Laws 1876, Ch. 122, Art. 14, Sec, 20.] In all cases where school lands fail to sell as provided for in this act, the county treasurer may dispose of said lands at private sale to actual settlers only, in tracts not exceeding one hundred and sixty acres to each purchaser: *Provided,* That no sale be made at less than the appraised value of the land and improvements: *And provided further,* That if school lands, once offered at public sale, are not sold within one year from the time of said sale, they shall be reappraised and sold at public sale, as other school lands are sold : *Provided further,* That the person so residing upon said school land shall have the privilege of purchasing said land, exclusive of the appraised value of the improvements; but in the event of any person other than the actual settler buying in said land, the person so purchasing shall pay to the person entitled to the pay for the improvements the amount of the appraised value of said improvements, they having been previously appraised according to the provisions of this act.

Privilege of School District.—SEC. 226. [Laws 1876, Ch. 122, Art. 14, Sec. 21.] Any school district shall be entitled to purchase and acquire, for a school-house site, any quantity of land, not exceeding two acres, of any school lands situate in such district, and shall acquire the title to the same according to the provisions of this act: *Provided*, That such tract shall be situate on one of the boundary lines of the section, or any quarter-section thereof.

Fees.—SEC. 227. [Laws 1876, Ch. 122, Art. 14, Sec. 22.] Each appraiser required under this law shall receive two dollars per day ; and, in cases when it is necessary to divide timbered lands into lots of less size than the legal subdivisions, the surveyor, chainmen and axmen shall receive the same pay as is provided for by law in other cases. The county clerk, under this act, shall be allowed for filing each paper, five cents; for recording each appraisement and other paper necessary to be recorded, seven cents per folio; for granting a certificate to a purchaser of school land, twenty-five cents; for indorsing payment on certificate, five cents; for filing treasurer's receipt, five cents; for approving bonds, twenty-five cents—to be paid by the purchaser; for making out abstract to be forwarded to auditor of state, five cents for each tract of land. The county treasurer shall receive for making out list of land for the printer, or to be posted, five cents for each tract advertised ; for issuing a receipt to purchaser of school land, twenty-five cents, which receipt, before it shall be of any validity, shall be presented by the purchaser to the county clerk, who shall indorse the same as entered upon the proper books of his office; on the net proceeds of the sale of school lands, one per cent.; and the county treasurer shall receive no fees for the sale of school lands except as provided for in this act. The printer, for publication of notice for sale of school lands, shall receive legal rates. The probate judge shall be allowed the same fees under this act as for similar services in his court. The county attorney, sheriff and district clerk shall receive for their respective services, under this act, the fees allowed by law for similar services. The several amounts above specified shall be paid by the county treasurer out of any money arising from the sale of the school lands, on the order of the county superintendent of public instruction ; and the county superintendent is hereby authorized to administer the oath to appraisers, and in verification of all bills presented to him he shall take the affidavit of the person or persons presenting such bills. The county superintendent shall be paid as is now provided by law.

County Superintendent's Abstracts.—SEC. 228. [Laws 1876, Ch. 122, Art. 14, Sec. 23.] The county superintendent shall, on the first Mondays of January and July, in each year, transmit to the auditor of state an abstract of the amount of each order given, and for what service, which amounts shall be credited to the treasurer of the proper county. The treasurer of state shall be the custodian of all bonds or securities on which moneys arising under the provisions of this act may be invested, and he is hereby required to give additional bonds, as the governor of the state shall direct.

State Auditor's Report.—SEC. 229. [Laws 1876, Ch. 122, Art. 14, Sec. 24.] That it shall be the duty of the auditor of state to incorporate in his annual report to the governor each year, by counties and in the aggregate —

First: The number of acres of land sold under the territorial government, and the amount paid into the school fund of the state for the same.

Second: The whole number of acres of school lands sold in each county since the admission of the state up to the first day of July preceding such report; the total amount of sales; average price per acre; the amount paid as principal; amount of county superintendents' order[s] allowed for expenses incurred in the sale of lands; and the amount of unpaid installments bearing ten per cent. interest.

Third: The number of acres of school lands sold in each county during the year ending the first of July preceding the annual report; the amount paid [as] principal; the amount of superintendents' orders allowed; the amount of installments unpaid on the sales for the year, and bearing interest.

Fourth: A statement of the amount of school lands forfeited in each county during the year ending the first of July preceding the annual report, showing the number of acres in each tract forfeited, the person by whom forfeited, and for what amount, distinguishing between the unpaid principal and the unpaid interest which fell due during the year.

County Clerk's Report.—SEC. 230. [Laws 1876, Ch. 122, Art. 14, Sec. 25.] That it shall be the duty of the county clerk of each county to furnish the state auditor the report named in the foregoing section of this act, on or before the first day of October in each year.

Trespass on School Lands.—SEC. 231. [Laws 1876, Ch. 122, Art. 14, Sec. 26.] If any person shall cut down, injure, destroy or carry away any tree or trees growing upon any school lands that are or may hereafter be set apart for the use of schools, or any other state institutions, or cut, destroy or carry away any wood, standing or being upon or growing on any school, college or university land, or shall dig up, quarry or carry away any stones, ore or mineral, lying or being upon such lands, the person committing such trespass shall be deemed guilty of a misdemeanor, and may be indicted and fined in a sum not less than double the amount of damages proved to have been committed, and not exceeding one thousand dollars, and confined in the county jail not less than one month and not more than six months.

Complaint of Trespass.—Sec. 232. [Laws 1876, Ch. 122, Art. 14, Sec. 27.] Whenever complaints shall be made, in writing and upon oath, to any justice of the peace, that any person has violated the provisions of the preceding section of this act, it shall be the duty of such justice to issue his warrant, under his hand, reciting the substance of the complaint, and commanding the officer to whom it is directed forthwith to apprehend the person so complained of, and bring him before such justice.

Procedure in Justice's Court.—Sec. 233. [Laws 1876, Ch. 122, Art. 14, Sec. 28.] Upon such person being brought before such justice, it shall be the duty of the justice to examine the complaint and the witnesses which either party may produce; and, if it shall appear to the satisfaction of the justice that the person complained of is probably guilty, he shall require such person to enter into recognizance in such sum, not exceeding two thousand dollars, with two or more sufficient securities, as such justice may direct, to appear at the next term of the district court; and in default of such recognizance, the justice shall commit such person to jail to await the action of said district court.

Grand Jury.—Sec. 234. [Laws 1876, Ch. 122, Art. 14, Sec. 29.] It shall be the duty of each court having criminal jurisdiction to give this act in charge especially to the grand jury at each term.

Complainants.—Sec. 235. [Laws 1876, Ch. 122, Art. 14, Sec. 30.] It shall be the duty of the county superintendent of public instruction, the district directors, clerks and treasurers, and all sheriffs and constables, to take notice of all trespasses committed on school lands in their respective counties, and immediately file a complaint against any person violating this act, before the proper authorities.

County Attorney.—Sec. 236. [Laws 1876, Ch. 122, Art. 14, Sec. 31.] It shall be the duty of the county attorneys in their respective counties to prosecute all persons charged with the violation of this act.

Fines.—Sec. 237. [Laws 1876, Ch. 122, Art. 14, Sec. 32.] All damages, fines and forfeitures collected under the provisions of this act shall be paid into the county treasury, for the use and benefit of the common-school fund.

Recovery of Forfeited Rights—Sec. 238. [Laws 1876, Ch. 112, Sec. 1.] That in all cases of the sale of school lands heretofore made, where the purchasers thereof have made partial payment or payments thereon, and have by law forfeited their rights to such lands, and the money already paid thereon, and when the said purchaser or purchasers have not been ejected, said persons, having made such partial payment or payments, their heirs and assigns may, within twelve months from the passage of this act, renew their right to retain the lands so forfeited by paying the amount due on said lands in the manner provided by exist-

ing law: *Provided*, That when such lands shall have been disposed of
to other persons under the law, no interest thereby obtained shall be
affected by this act: *And provided further*, That all expenses that may
be incurred under this act shall be borne by those seeking to avail themselves of the benefits of this act.

Report of Sales; Penalty.—SEC. 239. [Laws 1876, Ch. 126, Sec. 1.]
That section two of chapter one hundred and thirty-nine of the laws of
eighteen hundred and seventy-one be and the same is hereby amended
so as to read as follows: Sec. 2. That it shall be the duty of the county
clerk of each county to furnish the state auditor the report named in the
first section of the act to which this is amendatory on or before the first
day of October in each year, and that upon failure to make said report
he shall be deemed guilty of neglect of duty and misconduct in office,
and shall be punished by fine not exceeding two hundred dollars, or by
imprisonment in the county jail not exceeding sixty days, or by both
such fine and imprisonment.

Duty of Auditor.—SEC. 240. [Laws 1876, Ch. 126, Sec. 2.] That it
shall be the duty of the auditor of state, on the thirtieth day of October,
or as soon thereafter as possible, annually, to report the failure and neglect of the several county clerks to make the required report to the
attorney general of the state, who shall at once institute the necessary
proceedings to punish said neglect of duty.

Payments, How Made.—SEC. 241. [Laws 1876, Ch. 127, Sec. 1.]
That section ten of chapter ninety-four of the general statutes of eighteen
hundred and sixty-eight be and the same is hereby amended so as to
read as follows: Section 10. The purchaser shall pay to the [county]
treasurer annually the amount of each yearly installment, with interest,
as specified in his bond, and the treasurer shall give duplicate receipts
to the purchaser therefor, stating the amount therein paid, and on what
account; one of which shall forthwith be delivered by the purchaser to
the county clerk, who shall credit him with the same, and charge the
amount to the treasurer.

Prosecution of County Treasurers.—SEC. 242. [Laws 1876, Ch.
127, Sec. 2.] That upon the failure of the several county treasurers to
pay into the state treasury the full amount received in their respective
counties from the sale of school lands, or the interest paid thereon at
each semi-annual settlement, it shall be the duty of the auditor of state
immediately to require the prosecuting attorney of the proper county to
prosecute the delinquent under the provisions of section thirteen of the
act to which this [is] amendatory.

ARTICLE XV.—STATE PERMANENT SCHOOL FUND.

School Fund Commissioners.—SEC. 243. [Laws 1879, Ch. 166, Sec. 113.] The state superintendent of public instruction, secretary of state and attorney general shall constitute a board of commissioners for the management and investment of the state permanent school, state normal school and state university funds. Such board shall be organized as follows: The secretary of state shall be the president of such board, and the state superintendent of public instruction shall be the secretary thereof. In the absence of either of said officers, the attorney general shall act as president, or as secretary, as the case may require. Such commissioners, when acting as such, must act personally. No member thereof can be represented in such board by any assistant or clerk in the office of which such member is the chief officer.

Meetings.—SEC. 244. Such board of commissioners shall meet regularly in the office of the state superintendent of public instruction, on the last Saturday of each month, at ten o'clock A. M. Special meetings of the board may be held at any time at the call of any member.

Records.—SEC. 245. [Laws 1879, Ch. 166, Sec. 114.] Said commissioners shall keep in a suitable book a full and correct record of all their proceedings at every session of the board, which record at the close of each session shall be signed by the president and secretary.

Bonds Offered.—SEC. 246. [Laws 1879, Ch. 166, Sec. 116.] They shall also keep such other books as may be necessary to properly register and describe all bonds offered to them, and all bonds bought by them for the benefit of the permanent school, state agricultural college, state normal school and state university funds, or either. Such record books shall be ruled so as to enable the board to register the name and residence of the person offering to sell any such bond or bonds, the name and residence or location of the owner or district for whom such offer is made, and a full, detailed description of every bond, whether United States, state or school-district, and the date, number, series, amount and rate of interest of each bond, and when the interest and principal respectively are payable; and such record shall be made of every such bond before the board shall act upon the question of purchasing such bond.

Investment.—Sec. 247. [Laws 1879, Ch.166, Sec.117.] Said board of commissioners shall have the power, and it is hereby made their duty, from time to time to invest any moneys belonging to the permanent school, state agricultural college, state normal school and state university funds in the bonds of the state of Kansas, or of the United States, and school-district bonds of the several school districts of the state of Kansas. In making such investments they shall give preference to the bonds of the state of Kansas and school-district bonds, whenever the same can be procured most advantageously to the said funds; but they shall not pay for any state or school-district bonds in any case a greater sum than the par value of the same, nor shall they pay for any such bonds any greater sum than the actual market price thereof at the time of purchasing the same.

Quorum and Business.—Sec. 248. [Laws 1879, Ch. 166, Sec. 118.] Any two members of said board shall constitute a quorum. But such board shall not purchase any school-district bond or bonds except at a legal session thereof, nor unless every member of the board is notified in time to be present at such meeting, and notified also that the question of purchasing such bonds is to be considered thereat, designating the bonds.

Records.—Sec. 249. [Laws 1879, Ch.166, Sec. 119.] Said commissioners shall keep a record showing a detailed statement of the condition of the state permanent school, state normal school and state university funds under their control, amount of each fund, how invested, when due, interest paid, and every other act in any manner connected with the management and investment of said funds; and the state superintendent of public instruction shall biennially report all such investments to the governor, to be laid before the legislature.

Office and Records.—Sec. 250. [Laws 1879, Ch. 166, Sec. 120.] All the records and record books of such board shall be kept in the office of the state superintendent of public instruction, but the same shall at all times be open for the inspection of every member of such board and other state officers, and any member or committee of the legislature or either house thereof.

Orders to be Drawn.—SEC. 251. [Laws 1879, Ch. 166, Sec. 121.] In the investment of the state permanent school, state normal school, and state university funds, the commissioners of these funds are hereby authorized to draw their order on the state treasurer, payable out of the fund invested, for the purchase price of the bond, and an order payable out of the annual fund for any accrued interest that may have accumulated on the bonds purchased; which orders, previous to their delivery, shall be registered by the state treasurer in a book provided for that purpose.

Custodian.—SEC. 252. [Laws 1879, Ch. 166, Sec. 122.] All moneys belonging to the state permanent school, state normal school, and state university funds, shall be paid to and held by the state treasurer, and be subject to the order of the board of commissioners. The state treasurer shall also be the custodian of all bonds, notes, mortgages, and evidences of debt arising out of the management and investment of the state school, state normal school, and state university funds, by said board of commissioners.

Collection of Moneys.—SEC. 253. [Laws 1879, Ch. 166, Sec. 122.] It shall be the duty of said board of commissioners from time to time, and as soon as may be practicable, to collect all moneys due and owing to the state school, state normal school and state university funds, and make investments of the same as hereinbefore required. If any such moneys shall remain unpaid for thirty days after the same become due and payable, the commissioners shall order the attorney general to proceed to collect the same by civil action to be brought and prosecuted in the name of the state.

Compensation.—SEC. 254. [Laws 1876, Ch. 122, Art. 15, Sec. 6.] Said board of commissioners shall receive such pay for their services as may be prescribed by law.

Unclaimed Estates.—SEC. 255. [Laws 1876, Ch. 122, Art. 15, Sec. 8.] In all cases where persons die without heirs and intestate, it shall be lawful for the superintendent of public instruction of the county where any land lies, belonging to the estate of such person dying without heirs and will, after a lapse of three years from the date of letters of administration upon such estate, to file a petition in the probate court of the county granting such letters, setting forth in said petition:

First—That such deceased person died without heirs, and intestate.

Second—That three years have elapsed since the date of the letters of administration.

Third—A description of the real estate.

Fourth — That no debts remain unpaid of this estate, not barred by the statute of limitation. Such petition shall be verified by the affidavit of the county superintendent of public instruction, or by some person who has knowledge of the fact.

Sale of Real Estate. — SEC. 256. [Laws 1876, Ch. 122, Art. 15, Sec. 8.] It shall be the duty of the probate court, on the filing of the petition mentioned in the preceding section, and being satisfied that the facts stated in said petition are true, to issue an order to the administrator to sell the real estate described in such petition, in the same manner as real estate is sold by administrators for the payment of debts due from deceased persons; and the same proceedings shall be had in confirming the sale and the execution of the deed by the administrator, as are provided by law for the sale of real estate for the payment of the debts of any deceased person. . ·

Proceeds of Sale. — SEC. 257. [Laws 1876, Ch. 122, Art. 15, Sec. 10.] It shall be the duty of the administrator, after the payment of the costs of said petition, and making said sale, and six per cent. commission to such administrator, to pay the county treasurer of the county where the land is situate the remainder of the purchase-money for the benefit of the common schools of the state, and shall take duplicate receipts therefor; and it shall be his duty to file one of such duplicates with the probate court of the proper county. If, at any time within twenty-one years after the date of payment of said money to the county treasurer, any person shall appear and claim said money as the rightful heir to said estate, and shall prove heirship satisfactorily to the probate court, the judge of said court shall so certify, and the state treasurer shall pay over to such claimant the sum so received from the county treasurer from such estate.

Consolidation of Bonds. — SEC. 258. [Laws 1876, Ch. 122, Art. 15, Sec. 11.] It is hereby made the duty of the school fund commissioners to consolidate all state bonds now belonging to or hereafter coming into possession of the permanent school fund, in the following manner, to wit: All bonds falling due on the same date and bearing the same rate of interest shall be consolidated into one bond, of equal amount to the bonds so consolidated, and coupons of interest shall be attached thereto, of equal amount to the consolidated coupons, and payable in the same manner as the coupons of the bonds so consolidated; such consolidated bonds shall be made out by the auditor of state, signed by the governor, and attested by the secretary of state, and shall be made payable to the permanent school fund of the state of Kansas, and shall have imprinted on their face the words, "Not transferable." All bonds presented by the school fund commissioners shall, in their presence, be canceled and destroyed by the auditor of state, after a consolidated bond shall have been issued for the same.

Registry of Bonds.—SEC. 259. [Laws 1876, Ch. 122, Art. 15, Sec. 12.] All consolidated bonds shall be registered by the auditor as other state bonds now are registered.

Registration.—SEC. 260. [Laws 1877, Ch. 172, Sec. 1.] Immediately after the passage of this act, it shall be the duty of the auditor of state to prepare a register of all bonds belonging to the permanent school fund.

Bonds to be Registered.—SEC. 261. [Laws 1877, Ch. 172, Sec. 2.] That it shall hereafter be the duty of the commissioners of the permanent school fund to present to the auditor of state all bonds which may hereafter be purchased by them prior to the deposit of the same with the state treasurer, and it shall be the duty of the auditor to register all bonds so presented.

Indorsement of Bonds.—SEC. 262. [Laws 1877, Ch. 172, Sec. 3.] That it shall be the duty of the auditor of state to indorse upon all bonds and coupons now belonging to the permanent school fund and deposited with the state treasurer, or which may be hereafter purchased by the commissioners of the permanent school fund, prior to the deposit of the same with the state treasurer, the following: "The property of and payable to the permanent school fund of the state of Kansas, and not negotiable or transferable," with his name thereto; and thereafter the said bonds shall not be transferable.

Treasurer's Statement.—SEC. 263. [Laws 1877, Ch. 172, Sec. 4.] That it shall be the duty of the state treasurer, immediately after collecting any interest on such bonds or the principal of the same, to file with the auditor a detailed statement or statements of the amount or amounts so collected, stating the name of the county, the number of the district, the number of the coupons or bonds paid by such district, and the amount paid; and the said treasurer shall cancel on the register in his office all coupons and bonds so paid.

Cancellation of Bonds and Coupons.—SEC. 264. [Laws 1877, Ch. 172, Sec. 5.] That immediately after the filing of such statement or statements by the treasurer, the auditor shall cancel such coupons or bonds as are designated in said statement or statements upon the register in his office, and charge the treasurer with the amounts.

Bonds to be Compared.—SEC. 265. [Laws 1877, Ch. 172, Sec. 6.] That it shall be the duty of the auditor of state, on the first Monday in August of each year, to compare the register kept by him with the bonds in the treasurer's office, and shall at the time of comparing such register require the treasurer to produce all coupons and bonds remaining un-paid, which shall be compared with the register.

Penalty.—SEC. 266. [Laws 1877, Ch. 72, Sec. 7.] That any state treasurer who shall fail or refuse to comply with the provisions of section three and section five of this act shall be deemed guilty of having converted the same to his own use, and shall upon conviction be subject to all the penalties provided for in section fifty-six of chapter one hundred and two, general statutes of the state of Kansas.

Time Extended.—SEC. 267. [Laws 1879, Ch. 160, Sec. 1.] The board of commissioners for the management of the state permanent school funds shall have the power, and it is hereby made the duty of said board, to exchange any school-district bonds belonging to the permanent school funds now in the state treasury for other bonds of the same district bearing a lower rate of interest and running a longer time than the bonds exchanged: *Provided,* That they shall not purchase any funding bonds running a less time than five years: *And provided further,* That the rate of interest on bonds running from five to fifteen years shall be seven per cent. per annum, and on bonds running longer than fifteen years the rate of interest shall be six per cent. per annum.

Payment before Maturity.—SEC. 268. [Laws 1879, Ch. 160, Sec. 2.] If at any time any board of education or school district shall have accumulated in the treasury sinking fund sufficient to pay in full any bond or bonds issued by such board or district before their maturity, the permanent school fund being the holders thereof, such board of education or school district may pay the same to the state treasurer and take up such bond or bonds; and the state treasurer is hereby authorized to receive the same and to cancel such bond or bonds, and the unmatured coupons attached thereto, and deliver the same so canceled to the officer paying the amount: *Provided,* That the state treasurer, before delivering said bond or bonds, shall present the same to the auditor of state, together with a statement showing the amount of coupons upon which no moneys have been received; and upon examining such statement, and comparing it with the coupons attached to such bond or bonds, the auditor shall credit the treasurer with the amounts shown to be canceled before maturity: *Provided,* That nothing in this section shall be construed to apply to bonds exchanged under the provisions of section one of this act.

Manner of Exchange.—SEC. 269. [Laws 1879, Ch. 160, Sec. 3.] The said board of commissioners, after having examined and accepted any funding bonds as contemplated in section one of this act, shall make a certificate in duplicate, directed to the state treasurer, stating that they have examined and accepted the funding bonds of school district number —, of the county of ——, or board of education of the city of ——, for the sum of —— dollars, in lieu of bonds numbered ——, for like amount issued by said district or board of education, now in the state treasury, and belonging to the —— fund, and that the treasurer of state is authorized to cancel and return the bonds so funded, together with the coupons attached thereto, and not matured, to the proper officer of the county, city or school district, which said certificate shall be signed by a majority of said commissioners, one of which shall be filed with the auditor of state and the other delivered to the state treasurer.

Records of Exchange.—SEC. 270. [Laws 1879, Ch. 160, Sec. 4.] Upon receiving the certificate as provided for in section three of this act, the state treasurer shall cancel the bonds described in said certificate, and shall write the word "Exchanged" and the date of such exchange upon said bonds, and shall make the same entry upon the register of said bonds in his office, and return such bonds so canceled to the proper officer, together with the coupons unmatured and attached to such bonds. The state treasurer shall, at the time of canceling such bonds, make a certificate directed to the auditor of state, stating the number and amount of each bond so exchanged and canceled, together with the number and amount of unmatured coupons attached to each bond. Upon receipt of such certificate the auditor of state shall compare the same with the certificate filed by the board of commissioners, and if found to be correct, shall cancel such bonds and coupons on the register in his office, and shall credit the treasurer with the amount of such bonds and coupons.

Funding Bonds to be Stamped.—SEC. 271. [Laws 1879, Ch. 160, Sec. 5.] All bonds accepted as funding bonds by the board of commissioners shall be stamped by the auditor and deposited with the state treasurer, and the auditor shall charge the treasurer with the amount in the same manner as though such bonds had been purchased for cash.

ARTICLE XVI.—STATE ANNUAL SCHOOL FUND.

Shall Consist of What.—SEC. 272. [Laws 1876, Ch. 122, Art. 16, Sec. 1.] For the purpose of affording the advantages of a free edu-

cation to the children of the state, the state annual school fund shall
consist of the annual income derived from the interest and rents of the
perpetual school fund as provided in the constitution of the state, and
such sum * as will be produced by the annual levy and assessment of one
mill upon the dollar valuation of the taxable property of the state, and
there is hereby levied and assessed annually the said one mill upon the
dollar for the support of common schools in the state; and the amount
so levied and assessed shall be collected in the same manner as other
state taxes.

State Treasurer.—SEC. 273. [Laws 1876, Ch. 122, Art. 16, Sec. 2.]
The state treasurer shall receive all the annual income of the state appropriated for the annual support of schools whether derived from the
interest of moneys loaned, rents of school lands, or annual tax, and hold
the same subject to the order of the state superintendent of public instruction.

Report.—SEC. 274. [Laws 1876, Ch. 122, Art. 16, Sec. 3.] He shall
keep in a separate book an account of all school moneys received by him,
distinguishing between the perpetual fund and the annual fund for disbursement, and shall report to the state superintendent on the first day
of February and first day of August of each year the amount of money
in his hands belonging to the permanent school fund and subject to investments, and on the first day of March and on the twenty-fifth day of
July of each year the state treasurer shall report to the superintendent
of public instruction the amount of money in the treasury belonging to
the annual school fund and subject to disbursement on the semi-annual
dividend.

Report.—SEC. 275. [Laws 1879, Ch. 166, Sec. 55.] . . . The
state treasurer shall also, on the fifteenth day of February and August of
each year, report to the state superintendent of public instruction the
amount of money in the treasury belonging to the annual school fund
and subject to disbursement on the semi-annual dividends.

Payment.—SEC. 276. [Laws 1876, Ch. 122, Art. 16, Sec. 4.] He
shall pay over to the treasurer of each county, on application, the amount
of school money due to said county, on order of the state superintendent
of public instruction.

Bond.—SEC. 277. [Laws 1876, Ch. 122, Art. 16, Sec. 5.] The state
treasurer shall execute to the state of Kansas a bond in double the
amount of money, as near as can be ascertained, to come into his hands
as treasurer of the school fund of the state, with sufficient sureties, to
be approved by the governor and superintendent of public instruction,
conditioned that he will faithfully discharge his duties as treasurer of
the school funds of the state. Said bonds shall be filed in the office of
the secretary of state.

County Treasurer.—Sec. 278. [Laws 1876, Ch. 122, Art. 16, Sec. 6.] The treasurer of each county shall apply for and receive of the state treasurer the school moneys apportioned to his county as soon as the same shall become payable.

Pay to the District Treasurer.—Sec. 279. [Laws 1876, Ch. 122, Art. 16, Sec. 7.] Each county treasurer receiving such moneys shall, upon proper application of the district treasurer of any district, pay over to the said district treasurer the amount apportioned to the district by the county superintendent.

Insurance Companies.—Sec. 280. [Laws 1876, Ch. 122, Art. 16, Sec. 8.] . . . . Every insurance company doing business in this state shall, in addition to the fees required by this act (chapter ninety-three, laws of eighteen hundred and seventy-one), pay into the state treasury, for the benefit of the annual school fund, the sum of fifty dollars each year.

ARTICLE XVII.—COUNTY SCHOOL FUND.

County Treasurer.—Sec. 281. [Laws 1876, Ch. 122, Art. 17, Sec. 1.] The county treasurer shall collect all moneys due the county for school purposes, from fines, forfeitures, or proceeds from the sale of estrays, and all moneys paid by persons as equivalent for exemption from military duty, and he shall, upon proper application of the district treasurer of any district in the county, pay over to the said district treasurer the amount apportioned to the district by the county superintendent. He shall also collect the delinquent taxes on real estate in any district, in the same manner as county taxes are collected, whenever such delinquent tax list shall have been lawfully reported and returned to him, and he shall pay the same over to the treasurer of the district to which such delinquent taxes are due; and if any county treasurer shall refuse to deliver over to the order of the county superintendent any school money in his possession, or shall use or permit to be used for any other purpose than is specified in this act, any school money in his possession, he shall on conviction thereof be adjudged guilty of a misdemeanor, and be punished by a fine not exceeding five hundred dollars, or by imprisonment in the county jail not [exceeding] one year.

County Clerk.—Sec. 282. [Laws 1876, Ch. 122, Art. 17, Sec. 2.] The county clerk of each county shall, on the first Mondays of March and July of each year, make out and transmit to the county superintendent a true statement of any county school money then in the county treasury.

Justice of the Peace.—SEC. 283. [Laws 1876, Ch. 122, Art. 17, Sec. 3.] Each justice of the peace shall report to the county superintendent, on the first day of March and on the twenty-fifth day of July of each year, the amount received from the proceeds of fines and estrays during the six months preceding, and belonging to the school fund of the county; and each justice of the peace, at the time of making his report to the county superintendent, shall promptly pay all of said proceeds to the county treasurer, to be disbursed by the county superintendent at the next ensuing semi-annual dividend.

Moneys and Property.—SEC. 284. [Laws 1876, Ch. 122, Art. 17, Sec. 4.] All persons having school moneys or other school property in their possession, by virtue of any act heretofore passed, are hereby required to pay over and deliver the same to the proper officers provided for by this act.

Compensation.—SEC. 285. [Laws 1876, Ch. 122, Art. 17, Sec. 5.] No county treasurer shall receive any compensation for disbursing or receiving either county or state school moneys.

Fine.—SEC. 286. [Laws 1876, Ch. 122, Art. 17, Sec. 6.] Any county treasurer who shall neglect or fail to pay over any school money in the treasury, on application, shall be subject to a fine of not less than five hundred dollars for every such neglect or failure.

Unclaimed Moneys.—SEC. 287. [Laws 1876, Ch. 122, Art. 15, Sec. 7.] If any sum of money directed by an order of the court to be distributed to heirs, next of kin or legatees, shall remain for the space of one year unclaimed, the executor or administrator shall pay over the same to the treasurer of the county for the benefit of common schools of the county.

Common School Fund.—SEC. 288. [General Statutes, Ch. 82, Sec. 332.] All fines and penalties imposed, and all forfeitures incurred, in any county, shall be paid into the treasury thereof, to be applied to the support of common schools.

ARTICLE XVIII.—COMPULSORY ATTENDANCE AT SCHOOL.

Children Shall Attend School.—SECTION 289. [Laws 1874, Ch. 123, Sec. 1.] That every parent, guardian or other person, in the state of Kansas, having control of any child or children between the ages of

eight and fourteen years, shall be required to send such child or children
to a public school or private school, taught by a competent instructor,
for a period of at least twelve weeks in each year, six weeks of which
time shall be consecutive, unless such child or children are excused from
such attendance by the board of the school district, or the board of
education of the city in which such parent, guardian, or person having
control resides, upon its being shown to their satisfaction that such
parent or guardian was not able by reason of poverty to clothe such
child properly; or that such child's bodily or mental condition has been
such as to prevent his attendance at school or application to study for
the period required; or that such child or children are taught at home
in such branches as are usually taught in the public schools, subject to
the same examination as other pupils of the district or city in which the
child resides; or that he has already acquired the ordinary branches required by law; or that there is no school taught within two miles by
the nearest traveled road.

Penalty for Violation of this Act.—SEC. 290. [Laws 1874, Ch.
122, Sec. 2.] Any parent, guardian or other person, failing to comply
with the provisions of this act, shall upon conviction be deemed guilty
of a misdemeanor, and fined in a sum not less than five nor more than
ten dollars for the first offense, nor less than ten nor more than twenty
for the second and every subsequent offense. Said action shall be prosecuted in the name of the state of Kansas before any court of competent jurisdiction; and all fines so collected shall be paid into the county
treasury for the support of common schools.

Duty of School Officers; Penalty.—SEC. 291. [Laws 1874, Ch.
122, Sec. 3.] It shall be the duty of any school director or president of
the board of education to inquire into all cases of neglect of the duty
prescribed in this act, and ascertain from the person neglecting, the reasons, if any, therefor, and shall forthwith proceed to secure the prosecution of any offense occurring under this act; and any director or president
neglecting to secure such prosecution for such offense within ten days
after a written notice has been served on him by any tax-payer in said
district or city, unless the person so complained of shall be excused by
the district or city board or board of education for reasons hereinbefore
stated, shall be deemed guilty of a misdemeanor, and liable to a fine of
not less than twenty nor more than fifty dollars, which fine shall be
prosecuted for and in the name of the state of Kansas; and such fine,
when collected, shall be paid into the county treasury as in section 2 of
this act.

Malicious Prosecution.—SEC. 292. [Laws 1876, Ch. 122, Sec. 4.]
That upon the trial of any offense, as charged herein, if upon such trial

it shall be determined that such prosecution was malicious, then the costs in such case shall be adjudged against the complainant and collected as fines in other cases.

<hr/>

ARTICLE XIX.—UNORGANIZED COUNTIES.

§293. Unorganized counties, where attached.   §296. Entitled to school funds.
294. Deputy superintendent and his duties.   297. Apportionment of school funds.
295. Penalty for failure to report.   298. Governed by general school laws.

Unorganized Counties.—SEC. 293. [Laws 1879, Ch. 159, Sec. 1.] All unorganized counties in the state of Kansas, by law attached to organized counties for judicial purposes, are and hereafter shall be attached to the same counties respectively for school purposes.

Deputy Superintendent.—SEC. 294. [Laws 1879, Ch. 159, Sec. 2.] The superintendent of public instruction in each organized county to which, by virtue of this act, any unorganized county is or may be attached for school purposes, shall appoint a deputy in such unorganized county, who shall attend to the organization of school districts in said unorganized county, subject to the approval of the superintendent of public instruction in said organized county. The deputy superintendent of public instruction in said unorganized county shall, within ten days after the time fixed by law for the report of the district officers in each year, make out and transmit in writing to the county superintendent of public instruction in said organized county a report containing a statement of the number of school districts or parts of districts in the unorganized county, and the number of children and their sex, resident in each, over the age of five and under the age of twenty-one years; a statement of the number of district schools in the county, the length of time a school has been taught in each, the number of scholars attending the same, their sex, the branches taught and the text-books used, the number of teachers employed in the same and their sex; a statement of the number of private or select schools in the county, so far as the same can be ascertained, and the number of teachers employed in the same, their sex, and the branches taught; a statement of the amount of public money received in each district or parts of districts; a statement of the amount of money raised in each district, and paid for teachers' wages, in addition to the public money paid therefor, for building, hiring, purchasing, repairing, or furnishing such school house, or for any other purpose allowed by law, in the districts or parts of districts, and such other information as the state superintendent of public instruction may require.

Deputy's Report.—SEC. 295. [Laws 1879, Ch. 159, Sec. 3.] Every deputy superintendent who shall neglect or refuse to make and deliver to the county superintendent of public instruction his annual report, as required by this act, within the time limited therefor, shall be liable to pay to the school districts in said unorganized counties the full amount of money lost to the said school districts by such neglect or refusal, with the interest thereon, to be recovered by the treasurer of said school district in the name of said districts.

Control of County.—SEC. 296. [Laws 1879, Ch. 159, Sec. 4.] The schools thus organized in said unorganized counties shall be under the control of the superintendent of public instruction in the said organized county, and the said superintendent of public instruction shall report to the state superintendent of public instruction the items reported by the deputy or deputies in said unorganized counties, and the state superintendent of public instruction shall apportion the state fund due the school districts in said unorganized counties to the county treasurer of the organized county to which said unorganized county is attached for school purposes, to be by him apportioned to the several school-district treasurers in such unorganized county or counties attached.

Apportionment.—SEC. 297. [Laws 1879, Ch. 159, Sec. 5.] The county superintendent of public instruction in such organized county shall draw on the county treasurer in his county for the amount due said school districts in such unorganized counties.

General Provisions.—SEC. 298. [Laws 1879, Ch. 159, Sec. 6.] The inhabitants of school districts in such unorganized counties shall hold their annual school meetings at the time prescribed by the general school law, and may hold special meetings as therein provided, and the qualified voters at such annual or special meetings shall have the same powers as are given by law to qualified voters at similar meetings of school districts in organized counties, and the duties and powers of school-district officers shall be the same in unorganized counties as are prescribed to be the duties of school-district officers by the school laws: *Provided,* That the provisions of article thirteen in the school law, being chapter one hundred and twenty-two, laws of 1876, and all acts amendatory thereto in relation to the issuance of school-district bonds, shall not be applicable to any school district in any unorganized county, nor shall the qualified voters or officers of any school district in any unorganized county have the right to levy tax or make any bonded debt.

ARTICLE XX.—PROVIDING FOR A FOUR-MONTHS SCHOOL, WHEN.

§ 299. Four months school required, if school
house be good.
300. Levy of tax for same; manner of.

§ 301. Failure of school board to hire teacher by
December 1, yearly; duty of superintendent in that case; provisos.

SEC. 299. [Laws 1881, Ch. 150, Sec. 1.] That in all school districts in this state in which there is a good and sufficient school building, a school shall be maintained for a period of not less than four months, between the first day of October and the first day of June in each school year.

SEC. 300. [Laws 1881, Ch. 150, Sec. 2.] Should the legal voters of any school district, at their annual school meeting, or special meeting called for that purpose, or the school-district board, neglect, refuse or fail to provide a sufficient levy of tax upon the taxable property of such district to maintain a public free school for a period of not less than four months in each school year, the county superintendent of such county shall, in conjunction with the county commissioners, immediately make an estimate of the amount necessary to support and maintain a public free school in such district for a period of not less than four months for the then ensuing school year, and certify the same to the county clerk of such county; and it is hereby made the duty of such county clerk to place the said levy upon the tax-roll of such county for that year, and such tax shall be collected at the same time and in like manner as other taxes are collected.

SEC. 301. [Laws 1881, Ch. 150, Sec. 3.] The county superintendent shall, upon the failure or refusal of the board of directors of any school district to provide and maintain such school as is provided by this act, on or before the first day of December of the current school year, hire a teacher or teachers for such school district, and provide the necessary fuel and appendages for the maintenance of such school or schools for at least four months during the current school year; and upon the close of such school and after the teacher of said school has made such reports of the same as provided by law, he shall certify to the treasurer of such district the amount due such teacher for his services, and also the amount due and the party or parties to whom due for fuel and other necessary expenses incurred in the support and maintenance of such school; and it is hereby made the duty of the treasurer of such district to pay, upon the order of such county superintendent, the amount or amounts found due by said county superintendent, and the filing of a sworn itemized statement of the several amounts so found due by such person or persons: *Provided,* That any qualified voter of such district is hereby authorized to bring suit against such county superintendent in the name of and in behalf of the district, for failure to comply with the provisions of this act; and all fines collected under the provisions of this act shall be paid into the county treasury for the use and benefit of the county school fund of such county: *Provided further,* That the provisions of this act shall not apply to those school districts which will be required to levy more than one per cent. to support and maintain such school as is provided for by this act.

INDEX.

DISTRICT OFFICERS — CONTINUED.

*9 7 8 3 3 3 7 2 3 2 4 7 4 *